the new granny square

the new
granny square

Susan Cottrell & Cindy Weloth

A LARK/CHAPELLE BOOK

A Division of Sterling Publishing Co., Inc.
New York

A Lark/Chapelle Book

Chapelle, Ltd., Inc.
P.O. Box 9255, Ogden, UT 84409
(801) 621-2777 • (801) 621-2788 Fax
e-mail: chapelle@chapelleltd.com
Web site: www.chapelleltd.com

Library of Congress Cataloging-in-Publication Data

Cottrell, Susan M.
  The new granny square / Susan M. Cottrell.
      p. cm.
  Includes index.
  ISBN 13: 978-1-57990-980-2
  ISBN 10: 1-57990-980-9
  1. Crocheting--Patterns. 2. Patchwork--Patterns. I. Title.

TT820.C845 2006
746.43'4041--dc22

                                                    2006001382

10 9 8 7 6 5 4 3 2 1

First Edition

Published by Lark Books, A Division of
Sterling Publishing Co., Inc.
387 Park Avenue South, New York, N.Y. 10016

Distributed in Canada by Sterling Publishing,
c/o Canadian Manda Group, 165 Dufferin Street
Toronto, Ontario, Canada M6K 3H6

Distributed in the United Kingdom by GMC Distribution Services,
Castle Place, 166 High Street, Lewes, East Sussex, England BN7 1XU

Distributed in Australia by Capricorn Link (Australia) Pty Ltd.,
P.O. Box 704, Windsor, NSW 2756 Australia

Manufactured in China

ISBN 13: 978-1-57990-980-2
ISBN 10: 1-57990-980-9

For information about custom editions, special sales, premium and
corporate purchases, please contact Sterling Special Sales Department
at 800-805-5489 or specialsales@sterlingpub.com.

table of contents

introduction

At first, the term "new granny square" may seem like a contradiction. After all, granny squares are as old as crochet itself, and the premise behind them—making something useful and beautiful out of scraps of this and that—is as old as womankind. Whether they evolved from purely economical reasons, or a creative soul with a hook in her hand deliberately began combining colors to make her work more lively and lovely, these beautiful multicolored squares and circles were a natural invention.

Even though the idea of granny squares is old, that doesn't mean today's designs are old-fashioned. This book's very definition of "granny square" thinks outside the, well, square. On these pages you'll find flowers, leaves, fluffy circles, and funky triangles as well—any motif that can be created as a single piece and connected together. The projects in this book are both new and familiar, from a hand-dyed silk ribbon scarf to chunky slippers to a beautiful skirt. Antique bed spreads and table covers that have long seen their usefulness have been recycled into new and up-to-date accents.

Today's wonderful array of yarns means nearly endless possibilities for crochet design. Wools, cottons, and acrylics are available in unusual beautiful colors and intriguing textures, from thick and nubby to delicate and silky. Unusual animal fibers such as Alpaca and Yak, and plant fibers like bamboo, corn, and soy, make for a most exciting and difficult task when choosing the materials for your creation. I can't even describe the options that my granny would find now if she could see them.

Crochet is not the exclusive skill of the granny, in the past or the present. Many people—both young and old, male and female—can enjoy this craft. It brings a wonderful sense of peace and comfort to sit and create a sweater, shawl, afghan, soft toy, or anything else, whether by the piece or as a whole.

A sense of calm sets in when one is crocheting that makes it such a delightful thing to do. I hope that you will enjoy this book and realize that the projects here are just a starting point to other creations that will bring the satisfaction and pride that comes from creating something yourself.

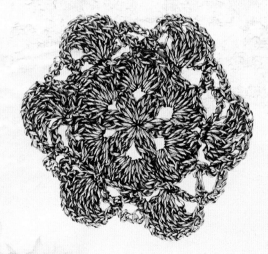

before you begin

understanding crochet

A strong foundation in any skill provides the ability to fly. Learning the basics and understanding the whys and wherefores of a craft allow one to move forward and tackle any new stitch or form with confidence. This book is not intended to be a primer—it includes both simple and complicated patterns—but I have included a few basic instructions that will serve as a reminder for the experienced and a guide for the novice.

Crochet, in basic terms, is the making of loops, using a tool with a hook on one end. By catching some string or yarn with the hook and pulling it through a loop repeatedly, you create a useful and decorative fabric. It is the way the loops are picked up, the winding of the string, yarn, or ribbon, and the number of loops used that come together to create the actual piece. Once the basic stitches are mastered and you understand how to combine and position them, you will discover how exciting and beautiful crochet can be.

gauge

Whenever you are following a crochet pattern you will notice that a gauge is included. This is an all-important guide to obtaining the proper size of the square or garment you are working on. If you don't get the proper gauge, the item will not fit properly and you may run out of yarn before finishing. Usually a swatch of stitching is made using the yarn and hook size suggested in the pattern. After making the swatch, usually a 4" square, lay it out on a flat surface and compare the size of your swatch to the one indicated in the pattern. If the swatch is larger or smaller than indicated, just change the size of the hook until you achieve the right gauge.

The gauge is the combination of the yarn size and the hook size. It is a stable measurement upon which a pattern is based, and is recommended with each pattern so that the results of your stitching will fit the pattern instructions and sizes shown. You will notice that each ball of yarn lists a recommended gauge to show the ideal size for that particular yarn. You can vary the yarn and hook as much as you want, but if you want to use the same pattern you will need to find the yarn and hook that will give you the same measurements. If you are working on your own design, the gauge will give you a starting place—a measurement on which to base your design.

varying patterns

In this book, you will find the same pattern appearing in several motifs. This shows the differences a change of yarn and hook size can make. We encourage you to try variations of the patterns provided. Vary the hook size to make the pattern looser or tighter (a larger hook will yield a looser weave; a smaller hook will yield a tighter weave). Combine thread, yarn, and ribbon sizes with each other, take pieces of one pattern and use it with another, vary what you see and use to make your own special pieces.

Perhaps you have found the greatest yarn and bought it without having a use in mind (as I have done many times). How do you find the best pattern for it? If the yarn has a lot of texture, experiment to see which size of hook and type of stitch would best suit the yarn. Work a single crochet pattern swatch, then use the same yarn and work it in a larger stitch and see the difference. Usually the more dynamic the yarn, the larger the stitch you will want to use to show off the fiber.

Yarns, threads, and ribbons have different weights, textures, and flexibilities. Consider this when using a pattern that needs a stiff fiber to give it shape, or a thinner yarn to showcase a pattern's intricate detail. Will the project need to have some resilience, such as a hat, a pair of gloves, or other clothing? Test your yarn or fiber to see if it has enough flexibility to be suitable for the project. Also consider laundering requirements when you are making a child's item of clothing or an afghan that will see a lot of use. The more an item is going to be used, the stronger you want the fibers and the stitch to be.

creating your own pattern

This book gives many more motifs and squares than patterns. With the right measurements and good swatches, you can create your own pattern from the squares, and determine the amount of yarn you will need. For a square or rectangular project, such as an afghan, decide the desired width and length of the finished project, then measure your sample square or motif. Divide the total length by the length of the square, then do the same for the width. Now you know the number of squares you will need. To determine the amount of yardage of each color needed, unravel the motif and measure the amount of yarn used for each color. Multiply the amount by the number of squares needed, and that will give you the total yardage for the project.

A more complicated pattern such as a child's sweater can be designed using a grid. Lay out the pattern on a piece of graph paper. You will need the size measurements of the item you wish to make and then the measurement of the square or motif that you will be using. If you are using a joining motif between squares, that measurement will also need to be added. This will give you the size of the square that will be represented on the graph. Plot out how you want the sweater to look, front (single or double-sided), back, and sleeves, then use the squares to tell you the number of motifs needed. Most sweaters are made up of rectangles and squares; if there is some shaping desired, you can determine this on the graph and you will know which squares need to be altered. Explore and enjoy, and always keep in mind that different factors will affect how your crochet pattern comes out, and that the gauge is important in determining how large or small the square or motif is.

This book helps explore possibilities. Study, look, learn, and transfer what you see to your hands. When you combine all that you have learned and go from there, you will realize that what you have learned is just the beginning and always will be.

the basics

basic symbols & abbreviations

-	previously made
( ) [ ]	repeat between
*	repeat; end of repeat
Beg	begin(ning)
Bet	between
Bpdc	back post double crochet
Ch-	chain previously made
Ch st	chain stitch
Ch(s)	chain(ing)(s)
Cl(s)	cluster(s)
Col	color
Dc	double crochet(s)
Dec	decrease
Dtr	double treble crochet
Ea	each
Hdc	half double crochet
Hk	hook
Inc	increase
Lp st	loop stitch
Lp(s)	loop(s)
Mod	modify(ied)
Patt	pattern
Pc	popcorn
Pl	pull(ed)(ing)
Rem	remain(ing)
Rep	repeat(ing)(s)
Rnd(s)	round(s)
RS	right side
Sc	single crochet(s)
Sk	skip
Sl	slip
Sl st	slip stitch
Sp	space(ing)
St(es)	stitch(es)(ing)
Tch	turning chain
Thr	through
Tog	together
Tr(s)	treble crochet(s)
Tr tr	triple treble crochet
WS	wrong side
Yo	yarn over

basic stitches

slipknot

1. Make a loose pretzel-shaped lp (A).

2. Insert the hk into the lp and pl both ends of yarn to close the knot (B). Be careful to not pl the yarn too tightly.

chain stitch (ch)

1. Place a slipknot on the hk. With hands in the correct position, and with the thumb and middle finger of the left hand holding the yarn end, wrap the yarn up and over the hk (from back to front) (C). *Note: This movement is called "yarn over" (yo) and is basic to every crochet stitch.*

2. Use the hk to pl the yarn thr the lp already on the hk (D). *Note: The combination of yo and pl the yarn thr the lp makes 1 ch st.*

3. Rep until ch is desired length (E). Try to keep movements even and all the ch sts the same size. Hold the ch near the working area to keep it from twisting. When counting sts, do not count lp on hk or slipknot.

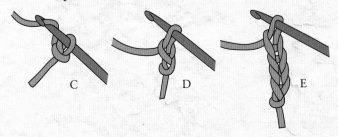

single crochet (sc)

1. Insert hk in indicated st (F) and yo.

2. Pl up lp (G) and yo. Pl thr 2 lps on hk (H).

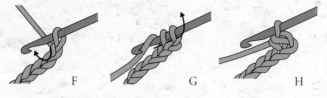

single crochet next 2 stitches together (sc next 2 sts tog)

1. (Insert hk in next st, yo, pl up lp) 2 times, yo, pl thr 3 lps on hk (I).

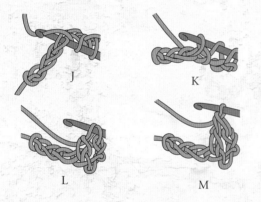

double crochet (dc)

1. Yo, insert hk in indicated st (J).

2. Yo, pl up lp (K). (Yo, pl thr 2 lps on hk) 2 times (L, M).

double crochet next 2 stitches together (dc next 2 sts tog)

1. (Yo, insert hk in next st (N), pl up lp, yo, draw thr 2 lps on hk) (O) 2 times (P, Q).

2. Yo, draw thr 3 lps on hk (R).

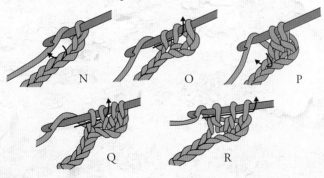

half double crochet (hdc)

1. Yo, insert hk in indicated st (S).

2. Yo, pl up lp (T).

3. Yo, pl thr all 3 lps on hk (U).

treble crochet (tr)

1. Yo 2 times (V), insert hk into fourth ch from hk (W). Yo and pl yarn thr ch. (4 lps on hk)

2. Yo, pl thr (2 lps on hk) 3 times (X, Y, Z). (1 tr completed)

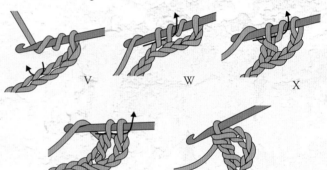

slip stitch (sl st)

Here, a slip stitch is used to join a ring.

1. Taking care not to twist ch, insert hk into first ch, yo, and pl yarn thr ch and lp on hk (AA). (Sl st completed)

2. To work sts in the ring, insert hk in center of ring and work around the base ch. Do not turn work when working in the rnd unless specifically told to do so to achieve a special effect.

Note: The sl st can also be used to join finished squares or to move across a group of sts without adding height to the work.

popcorn stitch (pc st)

1. Work specified number of sts in same st, pl up 1 lp in last st of group and drop lp from hk, insert hk in first st of group, and pick up dropped lp (BB).

2. Pl yarn thr and tighten, ch 1 to close pc (CC).

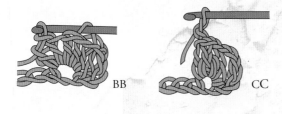

special stitches

long-dc

Note: This is a normal dc worked in a st or sp lower than rnd just previously worked. Because it is worked in a lower rnd, the dc threads are longer than usual. Yo, pl a lp thr required st in rnds below, (yo, pl thr 2 lps on hk) 2 times.

double treble crochet (dtr)

Yo 3 times, insert hk in required st, pl up 1 lp, (yo, pl thr 2 lps on hk) 4 times.

triple treble crochet (tr tr)

Yo 4 times, insert hk in required st, pl up 1 lp, (yo, pl thr 2 lps on hk) 5 times.

2 dc cluster (2 dc cl)

(Yo, insert hk in required st, pl up 1 lp, yo, pl thr 2 lps on hk) 2 times, yo, pl thr all 3 lps on hk.

3 dc cluster (3 dc cl)

(Yo, insert hk in required st, pl up 1 lp, yo, pl thr 2 lps on hk) 3 times, yo, pl thr all 4 lps on hk.

4 dc cluster (4 dc cl)

(Yo, insert hk in required st, pl up 1 lp, yo, pl thr 2 lps on hk) 4 times, yo, pl thr all 5 lps on hk.

3 dc puff

3 dc in required st, remove hk, insert hk in top of first dc, hk yarn and pl thr to form 1 puff st.

4 dc popcorn (4 dc pc)

4 dc in required st, remove hk, insert hk in top of first dc, hk yarn and pl thr to form 1 pc st.

5 dc popcorn (5 dc pc)

5 dc in required st, remove hk, insert hk in top of first dc, hk yarn and pl thr to form 1 pc st.

tr popcorn (tr pc)

3 tr in same required sp, remove hk, insert hk in top of first tr, pl yarn thr and tighten.

modified 4 dc cluster (mod 4 dc cl)

(Yo, pl 1 lp thr next st, yo, pl thr 2 lps on hk, yo, pl 1 lp thr same st, yo, pl thr 2 lps on hk) 2 times, yo, pl thr all 5 lps on hk.

7 dc popcorn (7 dc pc)

Work 7 dc in next st, remove hk, insert hk in top of beg dc, pl yarn thr. *Note: A ch-3 may count as the beg dc st.*

mod puff st

(Yo, insert hk under 2 dc, pl up 1 lp) 3 times, yo, pl thr 7 lps on hk, ch 1 to close.

afghan stitch (afghan st)

The first row of afghan st is worked in top lp of the ch st. Insert hk into second ch from hk and pl 1 lp thr—do not work off the lp. Insert hk into next ch st and pl 1 lp thr—again do not work off the lp. *Note: The whole row of ch sts are worked this way, accumulating 1 lp on the hk for ea st worked.* When the last ch st has been worked at the end of the row, yo and work 1 lp off hk. Continue to yo and work lps off hk 2 at a time until the whole row has been worked off and only 1 lp rem on the hk. (1 row completed)

Succeeding rows of afghan st are worked the same way, except the yarn is inserted into the vertical bar that occurs in front of ea st, and not into the top lps of the st. Be certain when working off the lps that the first lp to be worked off is worked off as 1 lp before beg to work off the rest of the lps, 2 at a time. If you fail to do this, the block will not be square.

11

back post dc (bpdc)

Yo, insert hk around the post of required st from back to front to back, yo, pl up 1 lp, yo, pl yarn thr 2 lps on hk, yo, pl yarn thr rem 2 lps on hk.

back post hdc (bp hdc)

Yo, insert hk around the post of required st from back to front to back, yo, pl up 1 lp, yo, pl yarn thr all 3 lps on hk.

long sc

Sc in next st 3 rows below.

lovers' loop (lovers' lp)

(Pl up 1 lp 1½", ch 1) 2 times, sc in next required st.

loop stitch (lp st)

Ch 1, (pl up 1 lp 1½", ch 1, sk next st, sl st in next required st) rep bet ( ) in required sts.

2-in-1 sc = dec st

Insert hk in required st, yo, pl up 1 lp, insert hk in next required st, yo, pl up 1 lp, yo, pl thr 3 lps on hk.

3-in-1 sc = dec st

Insert hk in required st, yo, pl up 1 lp, (insert hk in next required st, yo, pl up 1 lp) 2 times, yo, pl thr 4 lps on hk.

2-in-1 hdc = dec st

Yo, insert hk in required st, yo, pl up 1 lp (3 lps on hk), yo, insert hk in next required st, yo, pl up 1 lp, yo, pl thr 5 lps on hk.

crab stitch (crab st)

Sc sts worked in a backward direction—to the right or counterclockwise.

joining in new yarn

If the patt requires that you fasten off somewhere and rejoin somewhere else, or if you need to beg an edging, you will need to join in new yarn. Insert the hk where indicated, then yo. Pl it thr to make 1 ch. If you run out of yarn and need to start a new skein, make the final yo to complete the st, then drop the old yarn and make 1 lp with the new yarn. Pick up the lp and pl it thr. Hold down the short ends until the next st has been worked. There is no need to make a knot.

fastening off

When you have finished working a crochet piece, you will need to fasten it off. After making the last st, cut the yarn, leaving a 2" end. Wrap the end over the hk and pl it thr the last st. Pl until the 2" end comes thr. Tighten if desired by gently pl on the end.

blocking

Once you are finished making a piece, it may need to be pressed or "blocked." One thing to make certain of is that you don't flatten the work. Check the yarn label to make certain it can be ironed. If so, the label should indicate what iron heat setting to use. Make sure to cover the work with a clean cloth and block the WS of the piece.

joining motifs

edge to edge seams

This type of seam joint produces an almost invisible seam and is a very common method of joining because of the flat seam it produces.

Use a blunt needle threaded with yarn that matches or blends well with the color of the pieces to be joined. (Ideally you will be using yarn from the project, however if the project yarn is bulky or difficult to work with using a needle, you will need to proceed with a matching yarn that is easier to work with.

Place crocheted pieces tog with RS facing each other, lining up the rows evenly to produce a uniform look from one side to the other when it is finished. Pin the sides tog to help keep the rows lined up if desired.

Beg at one end of the motif/square. Insert the threaded needle under a strand of yarn on one side, cross over to the other side and pick up a strand of yarn (lp) there, rep up the side to the end. To contain the ends of the yarn at the beg, carry the tail 2"–3" up the side and st over it as you move up the seam. At the finish weave the end into the st just made.

backstitch seam

This is a good seam to use when the edge of the piece contains inc or dec. Use a threaded blunt needle and work small even backstitches as close to the edge as possible. Prepare the project as mentioned above and begin by securing the yarn to the edge of the fabric with several over cast sts. Make each st by reinserting the needle back into the fabric at the same point where it just came and passing the needle forward a short distance.

slip stitch seam

This is a very quick way to join your pieces. Use a crochet hk one or two sizes smaller than that used for the project. Insert the hk thr both sides of the work, ea facing RS tog. Draw thr a lp, insert the hk thr again and pull a second lp thr the fabric and thr the lp on the hk. Continue in this manner until you have finished the seam. Beg and end the yarn by weaving the tails thr the st in the seams.

chapter 1:
granny squares & motifs

This chapter includes examples of traditional granny squares and motifs as well as variations and unique designs. One of the fun things about crochet is the wide variety that you can create by varying basic stitches with different hooks and fibers. Several projects in this chapter demonstrate variations on the same pattern, and in fact, all of the patterns given have the ability to look different through experimentation and creativity.

basic granny block

materials
- sport weight cotton yarn
- size F hook, or size required to obtain gauge

gauge
finished block = 5" x 5"

directions
Ch 4, sl st in beg ch to form a ring.

Rnd 1: Ch 6, (3 dc in center of ring, ch 3) 3 times, 2 dc in ring, sl st in third ch of beg ch-6.

Rnd 2: Sl st in next 2 ch, ch 6, 3 dc in same sp, (ch 1, 3 dc, ch 3, 3 dc in next sp) 3 times, ch 1, 2 dc in same sp as beg, sl st in third ch of beg ch-6.

Rnd 3: Sl st in next 2 ch, ch 6, 3 dc in same sp, [ch 1, 3 dc in next ch-1 sp, ch 1,* (3 dc, ch 3, 3 dc) in next st], rep bet [ ] 3 times, end last rep at *, 2 dc in same sp as beg, sl st in third ch of beg ch-6.

Rnd 4: Sl st in next 2 ch, ch 6, 3 dc in same sp, [(ch 1, 3 dc in next ch-1 sp) 2 times, ch 1,* (3 dc, ch 3, 3 dc) in next ch-3 corner sp], rep bet [ ] 3 times, end last rep at *, 2 dc in same sp as beg, sl st in third ch of beg ch-6. Leave an 18" or appropriate length tail for sewing. Fasten off.

Note: If using the basic granny block patt and a larger block is needed, work additional rnds in the same manner, having 1 more 3-dc section bet ea corner. This block is designed to end at the corner to make sewing blocks tog easier. Notice Rnd 4 allows you to leave a tail for sewing purposes. To st 2 sides of the block, 18" will be enough.

gauge
finished block = approx. 4½" x 4½"

chain net block

materials
• cashmere/lambswool/nylon/silk yarn
• size H hook, or size required to obtain gauge

directions
Ch 5, sl st into beg ch to form a ring.

Rnd 1: Ch 3, dc in ring, (ch 5, 2 dc in ring) 3 times, ch 5, sl st in third ch of beg ch-3.

Rnd 2: [Ch 4, sl st in next dc, (sc, 2 hdc, 2 dc, 2 tr, 2 dc, 2 hdc, sc) in ch-5 lp (petal), sl st in next dc], rep bet [ ] 3 times.

Rnd 3: (4 sc in ch-4 lp, ch 5 (carry the ch-5 across front of next petal)) 4 times, sl st in beg sc, sl st in second sc, sl st in third sc.

Rnd 4: [Ch 4, (tr, ch 2, dc, ch 3, dc, ch 2, tr) bet 2 trs in center of petal of Rnd 2, ch 4, sl st in third sc of next sc-group of Rnd 3], rep bet [ ] 3 times. Fasten off.

tropical orange variegated square

gauge
finished block = 6½" x 6½"

special stitches
dtr
long dc

materials
- acrylic/cotton/viscose yarn in color B
- dk weight wool yarn in color A
- novelty polyamide blend yarn in color C
- size E hook and size H hook, or size required to obtain gauge
- sport weight acrylic yarn in color D

directions

Using size E hk and col A, ch 6, sl st in beg ch to form a ring.

Rnd 1: Ch 3, 2 dc in ring, (ch 3, 3 dc in ring) 3 times, ch 3, sl st in third ch of beg ch-3. Fasten off.

Rnd 2: Using col B, join with sl st in any ch-3 sp, ch 3, 2 dc in same ch-3 sp, (ch 1, 3 dc, ch 2, 3 dc) in next ch-3 sp 3 times, ch 1, 3 dc in next (beg) ch-3 sp, ch 2, sl st in third ch of beg ch-3.

Rnd 3: Ch 4, 3 dc in ch-1 sp, ch 3, (2 sc in ch-2 sp, ch 3, 3 dc in ch-1 sp, ch 3) 3 times, sc in ch-3 sp, sl st into first ch of beg ch-4. Fasten off.

Rnd 4: Using col C, join with sl st in first dc of any 3 dc group of Rnd 3, ch 3, 2 dc in same st, [work 3 dtr in ch-1 sp of Rnd 2 covering center st in rnd below (the second dtr of this group is the corner st), 3 dc in third dc of same dc group of Rnd 3, ch 1, sc in back lp only of ea of next 3 ch of Rnd 3, 2 long dc in ch-3 sp of Rnd 2, sc in back lp only of ea of next 3 ch of Rnd 3, ch 1,* 3 dc in first dc of next dc group of Rnd 3], rep bet [ ] 3 times, end last rep at *, sl st in third ch of beg ch-3. Fasten off.

Rnd 5: Using size H hk and col B, join with sl st in any corner dtr st, ch 3, 2 dc in same sp, [ch 1, sk 5 sts, 3 dc in second sc of next sc group, ch 1, sk 4 sts, 3 dc in second sc of next sc group, ch 1, sk 5 sts, (3 dc, ch 3,* 3 dc) in next corner dtr st], rep bet [ ] 3 times, end last rep at *, end sl st in third ch of beg ch-3. Fasten off.

Rnd 6: Using col D, join thread in any ch-3 corner sp, ch 3, 2 dc in same sp, [(ch 1, 3 dc in next ch-1 sp) 3 times, ch 1,* (3 dc, ch 3, 3 dc) in next ch-3 corner sp] rep bet [ ] 3 times, end last rep at *, 3 dc in same sp as beg, ch 3, sl st in third ch of beg ch-3. If sewing blocks tog, leave an 18" or appropriate length tail for sewing. Fasten off.

triangle

materials

- acrylic/cotton/viscose yarn in color C
- novelty polyamide blend yarn in color A
- polyester "suede" yarn in color B
- size G hook, or size required to obtain gauge

directions

Using col A, ch 4, sl st in beg ch to form a ring.

Rnd 1: Ch 3, dc in center of ring, [ch 1, 2 dc in ring, ch 3,* 2 dc in ring], rep bet [ ] 2 times, end last rep at *, sl st in third ch of beg ch-3. Fasten off.

Rnd 2: Using col B, join with sl st in any ch-3 lp, ch 2, 2 hdc in same ch-3 lp, [ch 1, 3 hdc in ch-1 sp, ch 1, 3 hdc in ch-3 lp, ch 2,* 3 hdc in same ch-3 lp], rep bet [ ] 2 times, end last rep at *, sl st into second ch of beg ch-2. Fasten off.

Rnd 3: Using col C, join with sl st in any ch-2 lp, ch 2, 2 hdc in same ch-2 lp, [ch 1, (3 hdc in ch-1 sp, ch 1) 2 times,* 5 hdc in ch-2 lp], rep bet [ ] 2 times, end last rep at *, 2 hdc in same ch-2 lp as beg, sl st in second ch of beg ch-2. Fasten off.

gauge

finished motif = approx. 4" each side

flower series

wild rose block

materials

- cotton crochet thread or lightweight yarn in color A
- cotton crochet thread or lightweight yarn in color B
- cotton crochet thread or lightweight yarn in color C
- cotton crochet thread or lightweight yarn in color D
- size E hook with crochet cotton thread, or size H hook with lightweight yarn, or size required to obtain gauge

finished block = 5" x 5" using lightweight yarn and size H hook

gauge

finished block = 4" x 4" using crochet cotton thread and size E hook

directions

Using size E hk and col A, ch 4, sl st in beg ch to form a ring.

Rnd 1: Work 12 sc in ring, sl st to front thread of post of beg sc.

Rnd 2 (Flower Center Loops): (Ch 2, sl st around post of next sc) 12 times. Fasten off.

Rnd 3: Fold center lps forward and work behind these lps in sc top of Rnd 1. Using col B, join with sl st in top of any sc of Rnd 1, ch 2, hdc in same st, (2 hdc in next sc) 11 times, sl st in second ch of beg ch-2.

Rnd 4 (Foundation for Spiral-type Petals): Ch 4, sk sc of Rnd 1 directly under the last 2 hdc just worked, sk next sc, [(pl center lps forward, sl st around the post of ea of next 2 sc made in Rnd 1, ch 4, sk next hdc of Rnd 3, sl st in next hdc) 3 times,* ch 4], rep bet [ ] 11 times, end last rep at *. Fasten off.

Rnd 5 (Petals): [Sl st into ch-4 lp, ch 1, (sc, ch 1) 6 times in same lp, sl st into ch nearest center of flower of ch-4 lp, ch 1, sl st in hdc of Rnd 3 on outside of flower bet ch-4 lps] 12 times. Fasten off.

Rnd 6: Using col C, join with sl st in any hdc where ch-4 petal lp is attached, ch 7, (sc in hdc where next ch-4 petal lp is attached, ch 6) 11 times, sl st into first ch of beg ch-7, sl st into second ch of beg ch-7, sl st into beg ch-7 lp.

Rnd 7: Ch 3, 2 dc in same ch-7 lp (first corner), ch 1, [(3 dc in next ch-7 lp, ch 1) 2 times, (3 dc, ch 3,* 3 dc) in next ch-7 lp (corner), ch 1], rep bet [ ] 3 times, end last rep at *, sl st in third ch of beg ch-3. Fasten off.

Rnd 8: Using col D, join in any ch-3 sp, ch 3, 2 dc in same sp, [(ch 1, 3 dc in next ch-1 sp) 3 times, ch 1,* (3 dc, ch 3, 3 dc) in next ch-3 corner sp], rep bet [ ] 3 times, end last rep at *, 3 dc in same sp as beg, ch 3, sl st in third ch of beg ch-3. If sewing blocks tog, leave 18" or appropriate length tail for sewing. Fasten off.

violet block

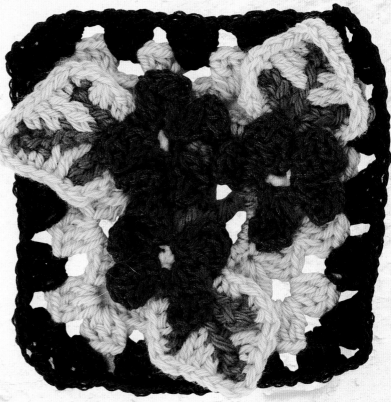

materials

- cotton crochet thread or lightweight yarn in color A
- cotton crochet thread or lightweight yarn in color B
- cotton crochet thread or lightweight yarn in color C
- cotton crochet thread or lightweight yarn in color D
- cotton crochet thread or lightweight yarn in color E
- size F hook, or size required to obtain gauge

special stitches

dtr

2-in-1 hdc (dec)

gauge

finished block = 5" x 5" using lightweight yarn

directions

Note: Make 3 flower centers with petals first, as the finished flowers are used tog in a later rnd.

Flower (Center): *Note: If you want the white center to be bolder, use 2 strands of thread for the center.* Using col A, ch 5, sl st in beg ch to form a ring. Fasten off.

Rnd 1 (Flower Petals): *Note: The petals are added onto the flower center in a counterclockwise direction RS facing.* Using col B, join with sl st thr back lp of any ch, [(petal beg) ch 3, 2 dc in same st, ch 2, turn, with WS facing, work a 2-in-1 hdc in 2-dc just worked, ch 3, sl st in third ch of beg ch-3 of petal, sl st in first ch of beg ch-3 of petal, remove hk, turn, with RS facing, insert hk thr back lp of Flower Center ch directly below petal, pl lp thr to the front of the flower petal (petal completed), ch 1, working counterclockwise sl st in back lp of next Flower Center ch], rep bet [ ] 4 times (5 petals on finished flower). Fasten off.

Block: When working with flowers, keep petals folded forward.

Rnd 1: With first flower RS facing, using col C, join with sl st in back lp of any Flower Center ch, (ch 3, sl st in back lp of next Flower Center ch) 3 times, mark last sl st made with a safety pin or yarn tie (connection point used later), (ch 3, sl st in back lp of next Flower Center ch) 2 times, last rep sl st is in beg sl st (joining sl-st).

Rnd 2 (Joining Flowers and Making Leaf Veins): *Note: Each flower has 1 leaf. This rnd makes the leaf veins and connects the flowers tog.* Sl st in next Rnd-1 ch-3 lp, [ch 7, sl st in fifth ch from hk, working toward the base of ch-7 sl st in next ch, ch 10, sl st in sixth ch from hk, working toward the base of ch-10 lp sl st in ea of next 2 ch, sl st in same Rnd-1 ch-3 lp, ch 7, sl st in fifth ch from hk, working toward the base of ch-7 sl st in next ch, sl st in same Rnd-1 ch-3 lp (veins of 1 leaf completed)], sl st in next Rnd-1 ch-3 lp, ch 4, tr in next Rnd-1 ch-3 lp, using

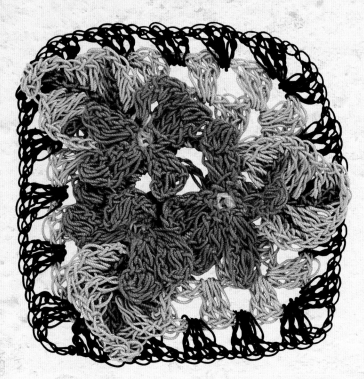

second flower, keeping petals folded forward, sl st in back lp of any Flower Center ch (joining sl-st), (ch 3, sl st in back lp of next Flower Center ch) 2 times, ch 1, turn, with WS facing sl st in ch-3 lp just made, turn with RS facing, rep bet [ ] finishing leaf veins, sl st in back lp of next Flower Center ch (base of ch-3 lp where second flower leaf veins are attached), (ch 3, sl st in back lp of next Flower Center ch) 3 times, last rep sl-st is in second flower joining sl-st, ch 1, turn with WS facing, sl st in ch-3 lp just made, ch 4, tr in next ch-3 lp, turn with RS facing, using third flower, keeping petals folded forward, sl st in back lp of any Flower Center ch (joining sl-st), (ch 3, sl st in back lp of next Flower Center ch) 3 times, ch 1, turn with WS facing, sl st in ch-3 lp just made, turn with RS facing, rep bet [ ] finishing leaf veins, sl st in back lp of next Flower Center ch (base of ch-3 lp that third flower leaf veins are attached to), (ch 3, sl st in back lp of next Flower Center ch) 2 times, last rep sl-st is in third flower joining sl-st, ch 1, turn with WS facing, sl st in ch-3 lp just made, ch 4, tr in next ch-3 lp, turn with RS facing, sl st in Rnd-1 marked sl-st to connect all 3 flowers. Fasten off. Be careful to keep all flowers RS facing and not twisted.

Rnd 3 (Finishing Leaves and Connecting Stems): This rnd sts worked in leaf veins are worked in back lps only. Using col D, join with sl st in Rnd-1 ch-3 lp just before first flower leaf veins, [ch 2, hdc in first ch of first ch-7 vein, 2-in-1 hdc in next ch, hdc in ea of next ch, sc in next ch, tr in second ch of second (ch-10) vein, dc in next ch, hdc in ea of next 2 ch, 3 hdc in ch at top of vein, hdc in ea of next 2 ch, sk 2 sts, dc in ch (across from dc on other side of vein), tr in next ch, hdc in fourth (top) ch of third ch-7 vein, hdc in ea of next 2 ch, ch 2, sl st in ch-3 lp at base of leaf], ch 1, 6 sc in ch-4 "stem" lp that connects to next flower, ch 3, keep ch-3 just worked behind the flower, sl st in ch-3 lp at base of leaf veins (just before the leaf veins)], rep bet [ ] 2 times, end last rep with sl st in beg sl st.

Rnd 4 (Block Behind the Flowers): *Note: This rnd is worked behind the flowers.* Ch 3, 2 dc in same st, ch 3, 3 dc in same st (corner), ch 1, 3 dc in second sc of next ch-4 stem, ch 1, (3 dc, ch 3, 3 dc) in second flower ch-3 lp bet stem connection point and leaf ch-3 (corner), ch 1, 3 dc in ch-3 lp at base of next leaf, ch 1, (3 dc, ch 3, 3 dc) in third sc of next ch-4 stem (corner), ch 1, 3 dc in sixth sc of same ch-4 stem, (3 dc, ch 3, 3 dc) in ch-3 lp at base of next leaf (corner), ch 1, 3 dc in fifth sc of next ch-4 stem, ch 1, sl st in third ch of beg ch-3. Turn, sl st in ch-1 sp just made, turn with RS facing.

Rnd 5: Ch 3, 2 dc in same ch-1 sp, [ch 1, (3 dc, ch 3, 3 dc) in next ch-3 corner sp,* (ch 1, 3 dc in next ch-1 sp) 2 times], rep bet [ ] 3 times, end last rep at *, (ch 1, 3 dc in next ch-1 sp), ch 1, sl st in third ch of beg ch-3.

Rnd 6: Using col E, join in any ch-3 corner sp, ch 3, 2 dc in same sp, [(ch 1, 3 dc in next ch-1 sp) 3 times, ch 1,* (3 dc, ch 3, 3 dc) in next ch-3 corner sp] rep bet [ ] 3 times, end last rep at *, 3 dc in same sp as beg, ch 3, sl st in third ch of beg ch-3. If sewing blocks tog, leave an 18" or appropriate length tail for sewing. Fasten off.

aster block

materials

- cotton crochet thread or lightweight yarn in color A
- cotton crochet thread or lightweight yarn in color B
- cotton crochet thread or lightweight yarn in color C
- cotton crochet thread or lightweight yarn in color D
- size E hook, or size required to obtain gauge
- size H hook, or size required to obtain gauge

directions

Using size E hk and col A, ch 4, sl st in beg ch to form a ring.

Rnd 1: Ch 1, 9 sc in ring, sl st around post of beg sc.

Rnd 2: (Ch 2, sc around post of next sc) 9 times, sl st in beg sc.

gauge

finished block = 5" x 5" using lightweight yarn and size H hk

Rnd 3: *Note: Work this rnd tightly.* (Sl st around post of next sc made by Rnd 2) 9 times, sl st in beg sl st. Fasten off. Turn over the center so the WS is up. *Note: This convex side is the RS.* Work additional rnds with RS facing.

Rnd 4 (Petals): Using size H hk and col B, join with sl st in any ch-2 sp of Rnd 2, ch 4, 2 tr in same sp, remove hk, insert hk in fourth ch of beg ch-4, pl lp thr and tighten (1 petal made), (ch 4, tr pc in next ch-2 sp) 8 times, ch 4, sl st in fourth ch of beg ch-4. Turn.

Rnd 5: Work 3 sl sts down the back of the second tr in the first petal to get to the base of the petal. *Note: This rnd draws the perimeter of the flower center tighter to make flower center pop up. Work this rnd tightly.* With WS facing (sl st in next sc of the flower center bet petals inserting hk from back to front) 9 times, end with sl st in beg sl st. Fasten off.

Rnd 6: Using col C with RS of flower facing, join with sl st in any ch-4 lp, ch 1, (8 sc in next ch-4 lp) 9 times, sl st in beg sc.

Rnd 7: Ch 3, 2 dc in same st (first corner), ch 1, [(sk 5 sts, 3 dc in next st, ch 1) 2 times, sk 5 sts, (3 dc, ch 3,* 3 dc) in next st (corner), ch 1], rep bet [ ] 3 times, end last rep at *, sl st in third ch of beg ch-3. Fasten off.

Rnd 8: Using col D, join in any ch-3 corner sp, ch 3, 2 dc in same sp, [(ch 1, 3 dc in next ch-1 sp) 3 times, ch 1,* (3 dc, ch 3, 3 dc) in next ch-3 corner sp] rep bet [ ] 3 times, end last rep at *, 3 dc in same sp as beg, ch 3, sl st in third ch of beg ch-3. If sewing blocks tog, leave an 18" or appropriate length tail for sewing. Fasten off.

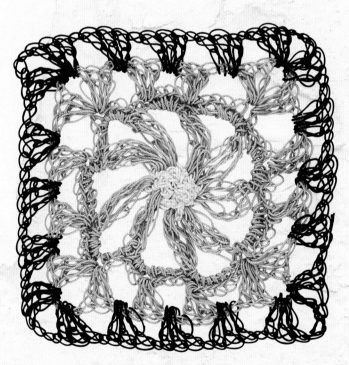

gauge

finished block = 4" x 4" using cotton crochet thread and size E hk

special stitches

tr pc

sunflower block

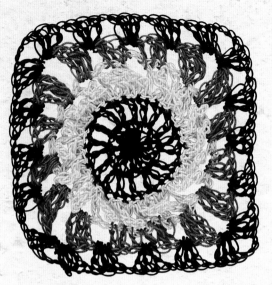

gauge
finished block = 4" x 4" using cotton crochet thread

materials
- cotton crochet thread or lightweight yarn in color A
- cotton crochet thread or lightweight yarn in color B
- cotton crochet thread or lightweight yarn in color C
- size E hook, or size required to obtain gauge

gauge
finished block = 5" x 5" using lightweight yarn

directions
Using col A, ch 4, sl st in beg ch to form a ring.

Rnd 1: Ch 3, 10 dc in ring, sl st in third ch of beg ch-3.

Rnd 2: Ch 4, [(dc, ch 1, dc) in next st, ch 1,* dc in next st, ch 1] rep bet [ ] 5 times, end last rep at *, sl st in third ch of beg ch-4. Fasten off.

Rnd 3 (Petal round): Using col B, join with sl st in back lp of any dc, [ch 5, sl st in back lp of second ch from hk, sl st in back lp of next ch, (sc in back lp of next ch) 2 times, (sl st in back lp of next ch from Rnd 2) 2 times (1 petal made)], rep from [ ] 15 times (making 16 petals), sl st in beg sp.

Rnd 4: Ch 6, (sk next petal, keeping petal to the front dc in back lp of second sl st bet petals, ch 3) 15 times, sl st into third ch of beg ch-6. Fasten off.

Rnd 5: Using col C, join with sl st in any ch-3 lp. Ch 3, [2 tr in same ch-3 lp, ch 3, 2 tr in next ch-3 lp, dc in same ch-3 lp (corner), ch 1, (2 dc, 1 hdc) in next ch-3 lp, ch 1, (1 hdc, 2 dc) in next ch-3 lp, ch 1,* dc in next ch-3 lp] rep bet [ ] 3 times, last rep ending at *, sl st in third ch of beg ch-3. Fasten off.

Rnd 6: Using col A, join with sl st in any corner ch-3 sp, ch 3, 2 dc in same sp, [(ch 1, 3 dc in next ch-1 sp) 3 times, ch 1,* (3 dc, ch 3, 3 dc) in next ch-3 corner sp] rep bet [ ] 3 times, end last rep at *, 3 dc in same sp as beg, ch 3, sl st in third ch of beg ch-3. If sewing blocks tog, leave an 18" or appropriate length tail for sewing. Fasten off.

pansy block

materials

- cotton crochet thread or lightweight yarn in color A
- cotton crochet thread or lightweight yarn in color B
- cotton crochet thread or lightweight yarn in color C
- cotton crochet thread or lightweight yarn in color D
- cotton crochet thread or lightweight yarn in color E
- size F hook, or size required to obtain gauge

special stitches

dtr

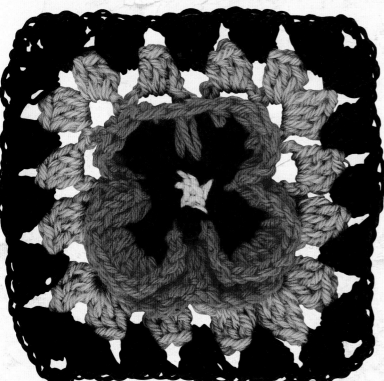

gauge

finished block = 5" x 5" using lightweight yarn

directions

Using col A, ch 3, sl st in beg ch to form a ring.

Rnd 1: Ch 1, 4 sc in ring, sl st around post of beg sc. Fasten off.

Rnd 2: *Note: Work this rnd in back lps only.* Using col B, join with sl st in any sc, ch 1, sc in same sp, 2 sc in next st, 3 sc in next st, 2 sc in next st, 2 sc in beg sp, sl st in beg sc. (10 sts)

Rnd 3: [Ch 3, dc in same st at base of ch-3, dc in next st, ch 3, sl st in same st, sl st in next 2 sc], rep bet [ ], ch 3, dc in same st at base of ch-3, 2 dc in ea of next 2 sc, dc in next sc, ch 3, sl st in same st. Fasten off.

Note: Each of Rnds 4–7 attach as a petal, and are not full in the usual sense. They were uniquely identified for ease of reading and following the patt.

Rnd 4 (back petal, across the top): Using col C, join with sl st in back lp of sl st directly across from where Rnd 3 was fastened off after the ch-3. Turn. *Note: The back petal is worked WS facing. This rnd is worked in back lp only.* Ch 4, 2 dtr in same st, sk ch-3, dc in next dc st, 2 dc in next dc st, sk ch-3, (3 dtr, 2 dc, 3 dtr) in center sl st, sk ch-3, 2 dc in next dc st, dc in next dc st, sk ch-3, 2 dtr in next sl st, ch 4, sl st in same st. Turn.

Rnd 5 (second petal, right top): With RS facing, ch 1, sl st in front lp of same sl st, ch 3, tr in same st, ch 1, dc in front lp of third ch of ch-3 of Rnd 3, 2 dc in front lp of ea of next 2 dc of Rnd 3, (dc, hdc) in front lp of first (top) ch of ch-3 of Rnd 3, hdc in back lp of ea of next 2 ch, ch 3, sl st in next sl st of Rnd 3. To position lp for next petal rnd, remove hk from lp, with RS facing, insert hk from back of flower to front on the right side of the post of the Rnd 2 sc directly below lp, pl lp to back of flower, remove hk, insert hk from front of flower to back, on the left side of post of the Rnd 2 sc, pl lp to front of flower, sl st in next sl st of Rnd 3 (directly above lp).

Rnd 6 (third petal, left top): Ch 3, hdc in back lp of first and second ch of ch-3 of Rnd 3, (hdc, dc) in front lp of next ch of ch-3 of Rnd 3, 2 dc in front lp of ea of next 2 dc of Rnd 3, dc in front lp of first (top) ch of ch-3 of Rnd 3, ch 1, sk rest of ch, tr in front lp of next sl st of Rnd 3, ch 3, sl st in next sl st of Rnd 3.

Rnd 7 (fourth petal, bottom): With RS facing and working along Rnd 3 on the bottom of the flower, sl st in Rnd 2 sc directly below lp, ch 2, 2 dc in back lp of ea of first and second ch of ch-3, dc in back lp of third ch of ch-3. Insert hk in back lp of next dc of Rnd 3, pl up a lp, yo, insert hk in next st, pl up a lp, pl lp thr all 4 lps on hk. Yo, insert hk around post of sc of Rnd 2 directly

below next dc of Rnd 3, pl up lp, yo, insert hk around post of next sc of Rnd 2 directly below next dc of Rnd 3, pl up lp, pl lp thr all 5 lps on hk. Yo, insert hk in back lp of next dc of Rnd 3, pl up lp, insert hk in next st, pl up lp, pl lp thr all 4 lps on hk. Dc in back lp of first ch of ch-3, 2 dc in back lp of ea of second and third ch of ch-3, ch 2, sl st in Rnd 2 sc directly below ch-3, sl st in next sl st of Rnd 3. Fasten off. Turn.

Rnd 8: *Note: This rnd will make 12 lps on the WS of the flower as a foundation for the next rnd to be worked on. The lps are anchored with sc in the center of pansy along each side, and just before the "corner" of the pansy, and just after the "corner" of the pansy. The "back" lps referenced in this rnd are lps on the WS of the flower—anchor points of the lps should not be visible from the front of the flower.* With WS facing and flower upside down, using col D, join with sl st in a sp made by inserting the hk underneath a thread of each of the posts of the center hdcs made on the Rnd 7 bottom petal, ch 6, sk 1 Rnd 3 st, sc in back lp of Rnd 3 dc, ch 6, sc in back lp of Rnd 3 second ch (corner lp), ch 6, sc in back lp of end sl st of Rnd 7, ch 6, sk 3 sts of Rnd 3, sc in back lp of dc of Rnd 3, ch 6, sc in second ch of Rnd 3 ch-3, ch 6, sc in back lp of center sl st of Rnd 3 bet top petals, ch 6, sc in back lp of second ch of Rnd 3 ch-3, ch 6, sk 1 Rnd 3 st, sc in Rnd 3 dc, ch 6, sc in back lp of beg sl st of Rnd 7, ch 6, sc in back lp of second ch of Rnd 3 ch-3, ch 6, sk 1 Rnd 3 st, sc in back lp of Rnd 3 dc, ch 6, sl st in beg sl st. Turn.

Rnd 9: With RS facing, sl st into next ch-6 lp, ch 3, 2 dc in same lp, [ch 1, (3 dc, ch 3, 3 dc) in next ch-6 lp (corner),* (ch 1, 3 dc in next ch-6 lp) 2 times], rep bet [ ] 3 times, end last rep at *, ch 1, 3 dc in next ch-6 lp, ch 1, sl st in third ch of beg ch-3. Fasten off.

Rnd 10: Using col E, join in any ch-3 corner sp, ch 3, 2 dc in same sp, [(ch 1, 3 dc in next ch-1 sp) 3 times, ch 1,* (3 dc, ch 3, 3 dc) in next ch-3 corner sp] rep bet [ ] 3 times, end last rep at *, 3 dc in same sp as beg, ch 3, sl st in third ch of beg ch-3. If sewing blocks tog, leave an 18" or appropriate length tail for sewing. Fasten off.

gauge
finished block = 4" x 4" using cotton crochet thread

sea green block

gauge
finished block = 6" x 6"

materials
- size F hook, or size required to obtain gauge
- worsted weight cotton yarn

directions
Ch 4, sl st in beg ch to form a ring.

Rnd 1: Ch 1, (sc in center of ring, ch 3) 4 times, sl st in beg sc.

Rnd 2: Ch 1, (sc, ch 3, 5 dc, ch 3, sc) in ea of 4 lps.

Rnd 3: Ch 4, tr in same st, [dc in next ch-3 sp, ch 3, sk next dc, sc in next dc, (ch 3, sc in next dc) 2 times, ch 3, sk next dc, dc in next ch-3 sp,* 2 tr bet next 2 sc], rep bet [ ] 3 times, end last rep at *, sl st in fourth ch of beg ch-4.

Rnd 4: Ch 4, [dc in next tr, 3 dc in next ch-3 sp, (2 dc in next ch-1 sp) 2 times, 3 dc in next ch-3 sp, dc in next tr,* ch 1], rep bet [ ] 3 times, end last rep at *, sl st in third ch of beg ch-4.

Rnd 5: Ch 4, 3 dc in same sp (corner), [hdc in next dc, sc in next 9 sts, hdc in next dc,* (3 dc, ch 1, 3 dc) in next ch-3 corner sp], rep bet [ ] 3 times, end last rep at *, end 2 dc in same sp as beg ch-4, sl st in third ch of beg ch-4.

Rnd 6: Sl st in next ch-1 corner sp, ch 3, sc in same sp, [(ch 1, sk next st, sc in next st) 8 times, ch 1, sk next st,* (sc in next ch-1 corner sp)], rep bet [ ] 3 times, end last rep at *, sl st in first ch of beg ch-3. Fasten off.

chunky block

materials

- 4-ply worsted weight acrylic yarn in color A
- nylon polyamide yarn in color B
- size F hook, or size required to obtain gauge

directions

Using col A, ch 4, sl st in beg
ch to form a ring.

Rnd 1: Ch 4, (3 dc, ch 1) 3 times in ring,
2 dc in ring, sl st in third ch of beg ch-4.

Rnd 2: Sl st in ch-1 sp (corner sp) ch 6, dc in same sp,
[sk next dc, 3 dc in next dc, sk next dc, (dc, ch 3, dc) in
next corner sp], rep bet [ ] 2 times, end sk next dc, 3 dc
in next dc, sl st in third ch of beg ch-6. Fasten off.

Rnd 3: Using col B, join with sl st in corner ch-3 sp, (ch
4, dc in fourth ch from hk, sc in next dc, sk next dc, 3
dc in next dc, sk next dc, sc in next dc, sl st in next corner sp) 3 times. Fasten off.

Rnd 4: Using col A, join with sl st in corner ch-3 sp, (ch
1, sc in same sp) 2 times, [ch 3, sc in next sc, ch 3, sk
next dc, sc in next dc, ch 3, sk next dc, sc in next sc, ch
3,* (sc, ch 1, sc) in next corner ch-3 sp], rep bet [ ] 3
times, end last rep at *, sl st in beg sc. Fasten off.

gauge
finished block = 4" x 4"

octagon block

materials

• #10 cotton crochet thread in color A

• #10 cotton crochet thread in color B

• size D hook, or size required to obtain gauge

directions

Using col A, ch 5, sl st in beg ch to form a ring.

Rnd 1: Ch 1, 8 sc in ring, sl st in beg sc.

Rnd 2: Ch 1, 2 sc in same st, (2 sc in next st) 7 times, sl st in beg sc.

Rnd 3: Ch 2, hdc in same st, (2 hdc in next st) 15 times, sl st in second ch of beg ch-2. (32 sts completed) Fasten off.

Rnd 4: Using col B, join with sl st in any hdc, ch 4, 4 tr in same st, (ch 4, sk next 3 sts,* 5 tr in next st) 8 times, end last rep at *, sl st in fourth ch of beg ch-4.

Rnd 5: Ch 1, sc in same st, sc in next 4 sts, (3 sc in next ch-4 sp,* sc in next 5 sts) 8 times, end last rep at *, sl st in beg sc. Fasten off.

peacock block

materials

• 4-ply sport weight cotton yarn

• size F hook, or size required to obtain gauge

directions

Ch 4, sl st in beg ch to form a ring.

Rnd 1: Ch 1, sc in center of ring, (ch 7, sc in center of ring) 7 times, ch 4, tr in beg sc. (8 lps completed)

Rnd 2: (Ch 3, sc in next lp, ch 5, sc in next lp) 3 times, ch 3, sc in next lp, ch 4 tr in top of tr. (Last corner sp completed)

Rnd 3: Working over side of tr just made, ch 3, 2 dc in corner sp, [ch 1, 3 dc in next sp, ch 1, (3 dc, ch 3, 3 dc) in next ch-5 sp, (corner)], rep bet [ ] 2 times, end ch 1, 3 dc in next sp, ch 1, 3 dc in same sp as beg of Rnd 3, ch 1, dc in top of beg ch-3 to complete corner sp. Leave a tail for sewing. Fasten off.

lime green round

materials
- cotton yarn
- size H hook, or size required to obtain gauge

directions

Ch 4, sl st in beg ch to form a ring.

Rnd 1: Ch 4, (3 dc in ring, ch 3,* dc in ring, ch 1) 4 times, end last rep at *, sl st in third ch of beg ch-4.

Rnd 2: Ch 4, 3 dc in next ch-1 sp, [ch 3, (dc, ch 1, 3 dc) in next ch-3 sp, ch 3,* (dc, ch 1, 3 dc) in next ch-1 sp], rep bet [ ] 4 times, end last rep at *, sl st in third ch of beg ch-4.

Rnd 3: Rep Rnd 2 except rep bet [ ] 8 times. Fasten off.

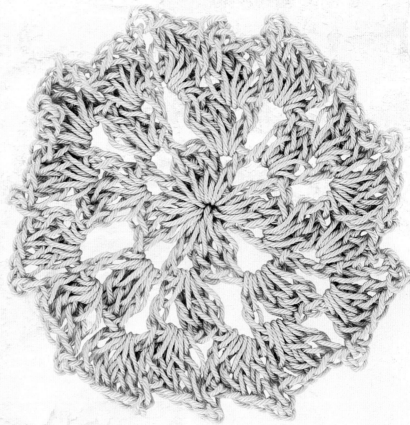

gauge
finished motif = 2" in diameter

five-petal flower

materials
- size G hook, or size required to obtain gauge
- acrylic/cotton/elastic/nylon worsted weight yarn

directions
Ch 8, sl st in beg ch to form a ring.

Rnd 1: Ch 3, 2 dc in center of ring, (ch 1, 3 dc in center of ring) 4 times, ch 1, sl st in third ch of beg ch-3. (5 groups completed)

Rnd 2: Ch 1, sc in last ch-1 sp, (ch 6, sc in next ch-1 sp) 4 times, ch 6, sl st in beg sc.

Rnd 3: Ch 1, sc in same st, (10 dc in next lp,* sc in next sc) 5 times, end last rep at *, sl st in beg sc. Fasten off.

eight-petal flower

gauge
finished motif = 4½" in diameter across at widest point

materials
- acrylic/cotton/elastic/nylon worsted weight yarn
- size G hook, or size required to obtain gauge

directions
Ch 8, sl st in beg ch to form a ring.

Rnd 1: Ch 3, 15 dc in center of ring, sl st in third ch of beg ch-3.

Rnd 2: [Ch 4, sl st in next dc, ch 4, (sl st, ch 8, sl st) in next dc], rep bet [ ] 7 times, end in same dc as beg ch.

Rnd 3: Remove hk, work behind lps just made, fold ch-8 lp forward, insert hk thr 2 lps (the first and last ch of ch-8 lp tog), pl thr these 2 lps, ch 1, sc thr same 2 lps, (ch 10, fold next ch-8 lp forward, sc thr first and last ch of this ch-8 lp tog) 7 times, ch 10, sl st in beg sc. (8 lps)

Rnd 4: Work (2 sc, hdc, 2 dc, hdc, 2 sc) in ea of next 8 lps, sl st in beg sc. Fasten off.

gauge
finished motif = 3½" in diameter

heavy cotton block

materials
- 16- or 18-ply heavy weight viscose yarn in color B
- heavy weight cotton yarn in color A
- size G hook, or size required to obtain gauge

gauge
finished block = 5" x 5"

directions
Using col A, ch 15.

Row 1: Dc in fourth ch from hk, dc in next 11 sts (13 dc counting beg ch-3). Turn.

Rows 2–6: Ch 3, dc in next 12 sts, turn, except after Row 6 fasten off.

Rnd 1 (Border): Using col B, join with sl st in top of last dc worked, ch 1, sc in same st (corner), work down side of dc [(2 sc in side of next dc, sc in top of next dc) 6 times, ch 1, sc in same st to complete corner, dc in next 11 dc, (sc, ch 1,* sc) in next dc for corner], rep bet [ ], end last rep at *, sl st in beg sc. Fasten off.

Rnd 2: Using col A, join with sl st in any ch-1 corner sp, ch 1, sc in same sp, [sc in ea sc to corner ch-1 sp, (sc, ch 1,* sc) in corner sp], rep bet [ ] 4 times, end last rep at *, sl st in beg sc. Fasten off.

ruffled flower

materials

- size H hook, or size required to obtain gauge
- worsted weight cotton yarn in color A
- worsted weight cotton yarn in color B

gauge

finished motif = 2½" in diameter

directions

Using col A, ch 4, sl st in beg ch to form a ring.

Rnd 1: Ch 1, 7 sc in ring, sl st in beg sc.

Rnd 2: Ch 1, sc in same st, (sc in next st) 6 times, sl st in beg sc.

Rnd 3: Ch 1, sc in same st (ch 7, sc in same st,* sc in next st) 7 times, end last rep at *, sl st in beg sc. Fasten off.

Work next rnd around the post of sc of Rnd 2, fold lps of Rnd 3 forward. Using col B, join with sl st around post of any sc of Rnd 2, (ch 3, 3 dc in same st, ch 3, sl st in same st,* sl st around post of next sc) 7 times, end last rep at * sl st in beg sl st (7 petals made). Fasten off.

spiral round

materials

- acrylic/wool yarn in color A
- acrylic/wool yarn in color B
- size G hook, or size required to obtain gauge

directions

Note: The rnds do not usually end at the beg of the rnd. Both col are worked at the same time without detaching.

Using col A, ch 4, sl st in first ch to form a ring.

Rnd 1: Ch 1, 7 sc in ring, remove hk but do not detach the yarn.

Note: Work rem rnds in back lp only.

Rnd 2: Using col B, join with sl st in beg ch 1 of Rnd 1, (2 sc in next st) 7 times, remove hk but do not detach yarn.

Rnd 3: Using col A, pl up lp, work 2 sc in beg st of Rnd 2, [(2 sc in next st) 2 times, sc in next st)] 4 times, remove hk but do not detach yarn.

Rnd 4: Using col B, pl up lp, work sc in next st, (2 sc in next st, sc in ea of next 2 sts) 7 times, remove hk but do not detach yarn.

Rnd 5: Using col A, pl up lp, sc in next st, 2 sc in next st, (sc in ea of next 3 sts, 2 sc in next st) 7 times, remove hk but do not detach yarn.

Rnd 6: Using col B, pl up lp, (sc in ea of next 4 st, 2 sc in next st) 6 times, end with sc in ea of next 6 sts, sl st in ea of next 2 sts. Fasten off col B.

Rnd 7: Using col A, pl up lp, sc in ea of next 2 sts, 2 sc in next st, (sc in ea of next 5 sts, 2 sc in next st) 2 times, end with sc in ea of next 3 sts, sl st in ea of next 2 sts. Fasten off col A.

string floral round

materials
- #3 cotton crochet thread
- size D hook, or size required to obtain gauge

directions
Ch 6, sl st in beg ch to form a ring.

Rnd 1: Ch 1, (sc in ring, ch 6) 5 times, sl st in beg sc.

Rnd 2: Sl st in next ch-6 lp, ch 1, (sc, hdc) in same lp, (ch 5, sc, hdc in next lp) 5 times, ch 2, dc in beg sc, to complete last lp and center next sts.

Rnd 3: Ch 1, sc, hdc in same lp, (ch 5, sc, hdc in next sp) 5 times, ch 2, dc in beg sc.

Rnd 4: Ch 2, hdc in same sp, (ch 5, 2 hdc bet next sc and hdc, ch 5,* 2 hdc in next lp) 6 times, end last rep at *, sl st in second ch of beg ch-2.

Rnd 5: Ch 1, 2 sc bet this st and next hdc, (4 sc in next ch-5 lp,* 2 sc bet next 2 hdc) 12 times, end last rep at *, sl st in beg sc. Fasten off.

little loop flower

materials
- #3 cotton crochet thread
- size D hook, or size required to obtain gauge

directions
Ch 5, sl st in beg ch to form a ring.

Rnd 1: Ch 1, 6 sc in ring, sl st in beg sc.

Rnd 2: Ch 1, 2 sc in same st, (2 sc in ea sc) 11 times, sl st in beg sc.

Rnd 3: Ch 1, sc in same st, (ch 6,* sc in next sc) 12 times, end last rep at *, sl st in beg sc. Fasten off.

gauge
finished motif = 2" in diameter

gauge
finished motif = 3¼" in diameter at widest point

open round

materials

- #8 cotton crochet thread
- size 6 steel hook, or size required to obtain gauge

directions

Ch 12, sl st in beg ch to form a ring.

Rnd 1: Ch 3, 4 dc in ring, (ch 12, 5 dc in ring) 3 times, ch 6, tr tr in third ch of beg ch-3.

Rnd 2: Ch 3, (2 dc, ch 3, 3 dc) in same lp, [ch 8, (3 dc, ch 3, 3 dc) in next lp] 3 times, ch 8, sl st in third ch of beg ch-3.

Rnd 3: Ch 1, sc in same st, sc in next 2 sts, (3 sc in next ch-3 sp, sc in next 3 sts, 10 sc in next ch-8 lp,* sc in next 3 sts) 3 times, end last rep at *, sl st in beg sc. Fasten off.

gauge
finished motif = 2¼" in diameter

cotton loop flower

materials

- #3 cotton crochet thread
- size D hook, or size required to obtain gauge

directions

Ch 5, sl st in beg ch to form a ring.

Rnd 1: Ch 1, 8 sc in ring, sl st in beg sc.

Rnd 2: Ch 1, (2 sc in next sc) 8 times, sl st in beg sc.

Rnd 3: Ch 1, sc in same st, (ch 8,* sc in next sc) 16 times, end last rep at *, sl st in beg sc. Fasten off.

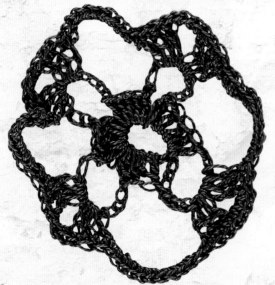

gauge
finished motif = 2½" in diameter

special stitches
tr tr

worsted round

materials

- size F hook, or size required to obtain gauge
- worsted weight acrylic yarn in color A
- worsted weight acrylic yarn in color B
- worsted weight acrylic yarn in color C

directions

Using col A, ch 4, sl st in beg ch to form a ring.

Rnd 1: Ch 1, (sc in center of ring, ch 5) 4 times, sl st in beg sc.

Rnd 2: Ch 1, sc in same st, (ch 5, sc in next lp, ch 5,* sc in next sc) 4 times, end last rep at *, sl st in beg sc. Fasten off.

Rnd 3: Using col B, join yarn with sl st in next lp, ch 3, (dc, ch 3, 2 dc) in same lp, (2 dc, ch 3, 2 dc) in next lp, ch 5, *(2 dc, ch 3, 2 dc in next lp), 2 times, ch 5, rep from * 2 times, sl st in third ch of beg ch-3. Fasten off.

Rnd 4: Using col C, join yarn with sl st in ch-5 sp, (ch 1, sc in same sp) 2 times, [(dc, ch 3, dc) in next ch-3 sp, sk next 2 dc, work a 3 dc cl in next sp, ch 1, sk next 2 dc, (dc, ch 3, dc) in next ch-3 sp,* (sc, ch 1, sc) in ch-5 sp], rep bet [ ] 3 times, end last rep at *, sl st in beg sc. Fasten off.

gauge
finished motif = 4½" in diameter

special stitches
3 dc cl

soft acrylic block

materials

- size G hook, or size required to obtain gauge
- soft acrylic yarn

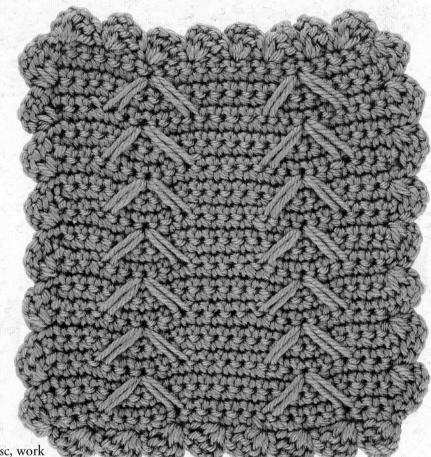

directions

Ch 25, turn.

Row 1: Sc in second ch from and in ea ch across (24 sc).

Rows 2–4: Ch 1, sc in ea sc, turn.

Row 5: Ch 1, sc in first 3 sc, [sk next 3 sc, work a long sc in next st 3 rows below next sc, sc in next 5 sc, work a long sc in same st as long-sc,* sc in next 5 sts], rep bet [ ], end last rep at *, sc in next 3 sc, turn.

Row 6: Ch 1, sc in ea sc across (24 sc), turn.

Repeat Rows 2–6 for patt until piece measures 6", end with Row 6. Do not fasten off, turn.

Edging: (Ch 3, 2 dc in same st (shell made), sk next 2 sts, sl st in next st) to corner. (8 shells) Work 8 shells along side, 8 shells along beg-ch end, 8 shells along rem side, sl st in beg st. Fasten off.

gauge

finished block = 7½" x 7½"

special stitches

long sc

fancy diamond

materials

- size F hook, or size required to obtain gauge
- soft acrylic yarn

directions

Ch 6, sl st in beg ch to form a ring.

Rnd 1: Ch 3, 8 dc in ring, ch 4, 9 dc in ring, ch 4, sl st in third ch of beg ch-3.

Rnd 2: Ch 1, [sc in back lp of ea of next 4 dc, ch 4, sk 1 dc, sc in back lp of ea of next 4 dc, 7 dc in ch-4 lp], rep bet [ ], sl st in beg sc.

Rnd 3: Ch 5, [7 dc in ch-4 lp, ch 5, sk 3 sts, sc in back lp of ea of next 4 sts, 3 sc in back lp of next st, sc in back lp of ea of next 4 sts], rep bet [ ], sl st in first ch of beg ch-5.

Rnd 4: Ch 1, [6 sc in ch-5 lp, sc in back lp of ea of next 7 dc, 6 sc in ch-5 lp, sc in back lp of ea of next 4 sc sts, ch 7, sk 3 sc, sc in back lp of ea of next 4 sc sts], rep bet [ ], sl st in beg sc.

Rnd 5: Ch 3, 2 dc in same st, [sk 3 sc, dc in back lp of ea of next 13 sts, sk 3 sts, 3 dc in back lp of next st, dc in back lp of ea of next 3 sts, 10 dc in ch-7 lp, dc in back lp of next 3 sts,* 3 dc in back lp of next st], rep bet [ ], end rep at *, sl st in third ch of beg ch-3. Fasten off.

gauge
finished block = approximately 5" x 6½"

little chenille flower

materials

- acrylic chenille yarn
- size F hook, or size required to obtain gauge

directions

Ch 4, sl st in beg ch to form a ring.

Rnd 1: (Sc in ring, ch 5) 5 times, sl st in beg sc. (5 petals)

Rnd 2: [Fold next petal forward, work (sc, ch 7, sc) in ring bet next 2 sc, which make the folded petal], rep bet [ ] around, sl st in beg sc. Fasten off.

gauge
finished motif = 2" in diameter

gauge
finished motif = 4" in diameter

special stitches
4 dc pc

chenille flower

materials

- acrylic chenille yarn
- size F hook, or size required to obtain gauge

directions

Ch 4, sl st in beg ch to form a ring.

Rnd 1: Ch 3, 2 dc in center of ring, ch 1, (3 dc in ring, ch 1) 3 times, sl st to top of beg ch-3.

Rnd 2: Sc (work backward) in last ch-1 sp, (ch 3, sk next dc, sc in next dc, ch 3,* sc in next ch-1 sp) 4 times, end last rep at *, sl st to beg sc.

Rnd 3: (Ch 7, sl st in same st, ch 3, work 4 dc pc st in next sp, ch 3, sl st in next sc) 8 times. Fasten off.

fluffy chenille block

materials
- acrylic chenille yarn
- size G hook, or size required to obtain gauge

directions

Ch 4, sl st in beg ch to form a ring.

Rnd 1: Ch 4, (dc in center of ring, ch 1) 11 times, sl st in third ch of beg ch-4.

Rnd 2: Ch 6, dc in same st, [sk next dc, (2 dc, tr, 2 dc) in next ch-1 sp, sk next dc,* (dc, ch 3, dc) in next dc], rep bet [ ] 3 times, end last rep at *, sl st in third ch of beg ch-6.

Rnd 3: Sl st in next ch-3 sp, ch 3 (2 dc, ch 3, 3 dc) in same sp, [ch 1 sk next 2 dc, (sc, ch 3, sc) in next dc, ch 1, sk next 2 dc, (3 dc, ch 3, 3 dc) in next sp], rep bet [ ] 3 times, end with sl st in top of beg ch-3. Fasten off.

gauge
finished block = 5" x 5"

pom-pom flower

materials

• dk weight bouclé wool yarn

• size F hook, or size required to obtain gauge

directions

Ch 4, sl st in beg ch to form a ring.

Rnd 1: Ch 1, (sc in center of ring, ch 8) 18 times, sl st in beg sc.

Rnd 2: [(Sc, hdc, 5 dc, hdc, sc) in next ch-8 lp, fold next 2 lps forward, sk this lp], rep bet [ ] 6 times, sl st in beg sc. Fasten off.

gauge

finished motif = 3½" in diameter

multilayer flower

materials

- #5 cotton crochet thread
- #10 cotton crochet thread
- size D hook, or size required to obtain gauge

directions

Motif: Using #5 thread, ch 3, sl st in beg ch to form a ring.

Rnd 1: Ch 1, 8 sc in ring, sl st in beg sc.

Rnd 2: Work this rnd in back lp only, work in spiral, mark beg of this rnd with safety pin, (2 sc in next st) 8 times.

Rnd 3: Sc in ea st around (16 sc, sl st in beg sc). Remove safety pin.

Rnd 4: Ch 1, sc in same st, ch 3, (sc in next st, ch 3) 15 times, sl st in beg sc. Fasten off.

Rnd 5: Using #10 thread, join thread with sl st around the post of any sc of Rnd 4, ch 1, sc in same st, [(ch 7,* sc around post of next sc) 3 times, sk next sc], rep bet [ ] 4 times, end last rep at *, sl st in beg sc (12 lps), sl st in next lp.

Rnd 6: Ch 1, (12 sc in ch-7 lp) 12 times, sl st in beg sc.

Rnd 7: Ch 1, sc in same st, sc in ea of next 5 sc, (ch 3, sc in same st,* sc in next 12 sc) 11 times, end last rep at *, sc in next 6 sts, sl st in beg sc. Fasten off.

Center Enhancement: *Note: This will look like a ch st covering sts already worked.* Using #10 thread, join with sl st around post of any sc of Rnd 4, sl st around post of ea sc of Rnd 4, sl st in beg sl st. Fasten off. Pl tail to WS and secure in place.

gauge
finished motif = 2½" in diameter

popcorn block

materials
- cotton crochet thread
- size G hook, or size required to obtain gauge

directions
Ch 4, sl st in beg ch to form a ring.

Rnd 1: Ch 3, work 4 dc pc in center of ring, ch 5, (work a 5 dc pc in center of ring, ch 5) 3 times, sl st to third ch of beg ch-3.

Rnd 2: [(Sc, hdc, dc, tr, dc, hdc, sc) in next ch-5 sp] 4 times, sl st to beg sc.

Rnd 3: Ch 4, dc in same st, [ch 5, sc in top of tr, ch 5,* (dc, ch 1, dc) bet next 2 sc], rep bet [ ] 3 times, end last rep at *, sl st in third ch of beg ch-4.

Rnd 4: Sl st in next ch-1 sp, ch 3, 2 dc in same sp, [ch 2, (5 dc pc, ch 2, 5 dc pc) in next ch-5 sp, ch 2 dc in next sc, ch 2 (5 dc pc, ch 2, 5 dc pc) in next ch-5 sp, ch 2,* 3 dc in next ch-1 sp], rep bet [ ] 3 times, end last rep at *, sl st in third ch of beg ch-3.

Rnd 5: Ch 3, dc in next st, ch 3, sl st in last dc (picot made), dc in next dc [(ch 3, sc in next ch-2 sp) 6 times, ch 3,* dc in next 2 dc, ch 3, sl st in last dc (picot made), dc in next dc], rep bet [ ] 3 times, end last rep at *, sl st to third ch of beg ch-3. Fasten off.

gauge
finished block = 4" x 4"

special stitches
4 dc pc

5 dc pc

tweed square

gauge
finished block = 5" x 5"

materials
- size F hook, or size required to obtain gauge
- sport weight silk tweed yarn

directions
Ch 7, sl st in beg ch to form a ring.

Rnd 1: Ch 3, 2 dc in center of ring, (ch 3, 3 dc in ring) 3 times, ch 3, sl st in third ch of beg ch-3.

Rnd 2: Ch 3, [2 dc in next dc, dc in next dc, (dc, ch 3, dc) in next ch-2 sp (corner)* dc in next dc], rep bet [ ] 3 times, end last rep at *, sl st in third ch of beg ch-3.

Rnd 3: Ch 3, dc in same st, [dc in next 2 dc, 2 dc in ea of next 2 dc, (dc, ch 3, dc) in next ch-3 sp,* 2 dc in ea of next 2 dc], rep bet [ ] 3 times, end last rep at *, 2 dc in next dc, sl st in third ch of beg ch-3.

Rnd 4: Ch 3, [dc in next 6 sts, 2 dc in next st, dc in next st, (dc, ch 3, dc) in next sp, dc in next st, 2 dc in next st,* dc in next 2 sts], rep bet [ ] 3 times, end last rep at *, dc in next st, sl st in third ch of beg ch-3.

Rnd 5: Ch 1, sc in same st, sc in next 11 sts, [(hdc, 4 dc, hdc)* 2 times in next sp (corner), sc in next 16 sts], rep bet [ ] 3 times, end last rep at *, sc in next 4 sts, sl st in beg sc. Fasten off.

eyelash trim block

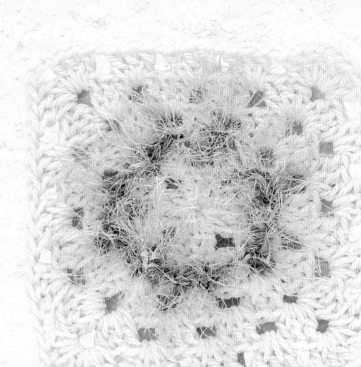

materials

- acrylic yarn in color A
- polyester eyelash yarn in color B
- size F hook, or size required to obtain gauge

gauge
finished block = 5" x 5"

directions

Using col A, work 4 rnds of basic granny block as follows:

Ch 4, sl st in beg ch to form a ring.

Rnd 1: Ch 6, (3 dc in center of ring, ch 3) 3 times, 2 dc in ring, sl st in third ch of beg ch-6.

Rnd 2: Sl st in next 2 ch, ch 6, 3 dc in same sp, (ch 1, 3 dc, ch 3, 3 dc in next sp) 3 times, ch 1, 2 dc in same sp as beg, sl st in third ch of beg ch-6.

Rnd 3: Sl st in next 2 ch, ch 6, 3 dc in same sp, [ch 1, 3 dc in next ch-1 sp, ch 1,* (3 dc, ch 3, 3 dc) in next st], rep bet [ ] 3 times, end last rep at *, 2 dc in same sp as beg, sl st in third ch of beg ch-6.

Rnd 4: Sl st in next 2 ch, ch 6, 3 dc in same sp, [(ch 1, 3 dc in next ch-1 sp) 2 times, ch 1,* (3 dc, ch 3, 3 dc) in next ch-3 corner sp], rep bet [ ] 3 times, end last rep at *, 2 dc in same sp as beg, sl st in third ch of beg ch-6. Leave an 18" or appropriate length tail for sewing. Fasten off.

Trim: Rnd 1: Using col B, join with sc in any corner ch-3 sp of Rnd 1, (ch 3, sc in ch-1 sp of Rnd 2 just before 3-dc group, ch 3, sc in same ch-1 sp on the other side of the 3-dc group of Rnd 2, ch 3* sc in corner ch-2 sp of Rnd 1), rep bet ( ) 3 times, end last rep at *, sl st in beg sc. Fasten off.

beaded flower motif

materials

- ⅛"-wide silk round cord
- ¼"-diameter round glass pearlized beads (19)
- 4-ply cotton yarn
- 10" strand of bronze seed beads
- metallic thread
- sewing needle and matching thread
- size F hook, or size required to obtain gauge
- size J hook, or size required to obtain gauge
- tapestry needle

directions

Note: Cord is used for the flower, yarn is used for the leaves, and metallic thread is used for dangling the round beads.

Flower Motif: Using size J hk and cord, ch 4, sl st in beg ch to form a ring.

Rnd 1: Ch 1, 12 sc in ring, sl st in beg sc.

Rnd 2: Work in back lp only, ch 4, (dc in next st, ch 1) 11 times, sl st in third ch of beg ch-4. Fasten off.

Large Leaf: Using size F hk and yarn, ch 15, sc in fifth ch from hk, sc in next 2 ch, hdc in next ch, dc in next 5 ch, hdc in next ch, 3 sc in last ch. Work up on opposite side of ch, sc in next ch, hdc in next ch, dc in next 5 ch, hdc in next ch, sc in next ch, sl st in next st. Fasten off.

Small Leaf: Using size F hk and yarn, ch 12, sc in fifth ch from hk, hdc in next ch, dc in next 3 ch, hdc in next ch, sc in next ch, 3 sc in last ch. Work up on opposite side of ch, sc in next ch, hdc in next ch, dc in next 3 ch, hdc in next ch, sc in next ch, sl st in next st. Fasten off.

Dangling Beads: String 7 round glass beads on metallic thread. Join with sl st to flower in top of any sc of Rnd 1, ch 14, sl up a bead and ch 1 beyond the bead, ch 4, sl up 2 beads, ch 6, sl st in center of dc below the sc first worked, ch 7, sl up 1 bead, ch 5, sl up 1 bead, ch 1, sl up 1 bead, ch 5, sl up the last bead, sl st in top of dc to left of last dc worked. Fasten off.

Center Decoration: Thread tapestry needle with metallic thread. Sew 12 round glass beads in center as desired. Make 4–5 lps with string of seed beads and tack in place. Knot well to fasten off.

Finishing: St leaves in place on left side of dangling beads.

gauge
finished motif = 3" in diameter; leaves = 2¼" x 2¾"

suede diamond block

materials
- cotton/rayon yarn in color B
- nylon "suede" yarn in color A
- size G hook, or size required to obtain gauge

gauge
finished block =
5½" x 7¾"

directions
Note: When changing col, the yarn is not fastened off.

Using col A, ch 6.

Row 1A: [Sl st in second ch from hk, sc in next ch, hdc in next ch, dc in next ch, tr in next (beg) ch], pl up lp about 2" long to avoid pl out sts, remove hk, do not detach yarn.

Row 1B: Using col B, join with sl st in beg ch of Row 1A, turn col B to WS, ch 6, rep bet [ ] of Row 1A, turn Row 1B crochet to WS, pl col A lp thr col B lp, tighten col B lp slightly, remove hk. Do not detach yarn. Turn.

Row 2A: Using col A, insert hk into lp, ch 4, [2 dc in top lp of other col tr, dc in top lp of each of next 3 sts, (3 dc, ch 1, 3 dc) in next st (corner), dc in each of next 3 sts, 3 dc in last tr], pl up lp about 2" long to avoid pl out sts, remove hk, do not detach yarn, turn, then rotate upside down. *Note: This will position you for the next row.*

Row 2B: Insert hk into col B lp, using col B, ch 4, remove hk and pl col B lp thr top ch of col A to secure sts tog. With hk inserted in col B lp, rep bet [ ] of Row 2A, pl col A lp thr col B lp, tighten col B lp slightly, remove hk. Do not detach yarn. Turn.

Row 3A: Insert hk into col A lp, using col A, ch 3, [2 dc in top of other col st, ch 1, (sk 2 sts, 3 dc in next st, ch 1) 2 times, (3 dc, ch 3, 3 dc) in corner ch-1 sp, ch 1, (sk 2 sts, 3 dc in next st, ch 1) 2 times], 2 dc in third ch of col B ch-3, ch 1, pl up lp about 2" long to avoid pl out sts, remove hk, do not detach yarn, rotate upside down.

Row 3B: Insert hk into col B lp, using col B, ch 3, remove hk and pl col B lp thr top ch of col A to secure sts tog. With hk inserted in col B lp, rep bet [ ] of Row 3A, pl col A lp thr col B lp, tighten col B lp slightly, remove hk. Do not detach yarn. Turn.

Row 4A: Insert hk into col A lp, using col A, ch 3, 2 dc in top of other col st, ch 1, [(3 dc in next ch-1 sp of other col, ch 1) 3 times, (3 dc, ch 3, 3 dc) in corner ch-3 sp, ch 1, (3 dc in next ch-1 sp, ch 1) 3 times], 2 dc in third ch of other col ch-3, pl up lp about 2" long to avoid pl out sts, remove hk, do not detach yarn, rotate upside down.

Row 4B: Insert hk into col B lp, using col B, ch 3, remove hk and pl col B lp thr top ch of col A to secure sts tog. With hk inserted in col B 2 dc in top of col A st, ch 1, rep bet [ ] of Row 4A, 2 dc in third ch of col A ch-3 below, pl col A yarn lp thr col B lp. Fasten off both col, leaving tails of 18" or appropriate length if sewing blocks together.

suede diamond half-block

materials

- cotton/rayon yarn in color B
- nylon "suede" yarn in color A
- size G hook, or size required to obtain gauge

directions

Note: Unlike the whole block, the yarn is fastened off when changing colors. This block would be used at the edge of a project that uses the whole blocks.

Using col A, ch 6.

Row 1: Sl st in second ch from hk, sc in next ch, hdc in next ch, dc in next ch, tr in next (beg) ch, fasten off. Turn.

gauge
finished block = approx. 4" x 5½"

Row 2: Using col B, join with sl st in top lp of tr, ch 3, 2 dc in same st, dc in top lp of ea of next 3 sts, (3 dc, ch 1, 3 dc) in next st (corner), dc in ea of next 3 sts, 3 dc in last tr, fasten off. Turn.

Row 3: Using col A, join with sl st in top of last dc worked in Row 2, ch 3, 2 dc in same st, ch 1, (sk 2 sts, 3 dc in next st, ch 1) 2 times, (3 dc, ch 3, 3 dc) in corner ch-1 sp, ch 1, (sk 2 sts, 3 dc in next st, ch 1) 2 times, 3 dc in third ch of other col beg ch-3, fasten off. Turn.

Row 4: Using col B, join with sl st in top of last dc worked in Row 3, ch 3, dc in same st, ch 1, (3 dc in next ch-1 sp of other col, ch 1) 3 times, (3 dc, ch 3, 3 dc) in corner ch-1 sp, ch 1, (3 dc in next ch-1 sp, ch 1) 3 times, 2 dc in third ch of other col beg ch-3. Fasten off, leaving a tail of 18" or appropriate length if sewing blocks together.

multipetal flower

materials

- #10 cotton crochet thread
- size 8 steel hook, or size required to obtain gauge

directions

Ch 5, sl st in beg ch to form a ring.

Rnd 1: Ch 1, 10 sc in ring, sl st in beg sc.

Rnd 2: Ch 3, dc in same st, ch 1, (2 dc in next st, ch 1) 9 times, sl st in third ch of beg ch-3.

Rnd 3: Ch 1, sc in same st, sc in next dc, (2 sc in next ch-1 sp,* sc in ea of next 2 dc) 10 times, end last rep at *, sl st in beg sc.

Rnd 4: Ch 1, sc in same st, (ch 6,* sk next st, sc in next st) 18 times, end last rep at *, sl st in beg sc.

Rnd 5: Ch 1, sc in same st, (8 sc in next ch-6 lp,* sc in next sc) 18 times, end last rep at *, sl st in beg sc. Fasten off.

gauge
finished motif = 3" in diameter

double petal flower

materials

- #10 cotton crochet thread
- size 8 steel hook, or size required to obtain gauge

directions

Ch 5, sl st in beg ch to form a ring.

Rnd 1: Ch 1, 10 sc in ring, sl st in beg sc.

Rnd 2: Ch 3, dc in same st, ch 1, (2 dc in next st, ch 1) 9 times, sl st in third ch of beg ch-3.

Rnd 3: Ch 1, sc in same st, sc in next dc, (2 sc in next ch-1 sp,* sc in ea of next 2 dc) 10 times, end last rep at *, sl st in beg sc.

Rnd 4: Ch 1, sc in same st, (ch 6,* sk next st, sc in next st) 18 times, end last rep at *, sl st in beg sc.

Rnd 5: Ch 1, sc in same st, (8 sc in next ch-6 lp,* sc in next sc) 18 times, end last rep at *, sl st in beg sc. Fasten off.

Rnd 6: Join with sc around the post of any sc of Rnd 1, (ch 4,* sc around the post of next sc) 10 times, end last rep at *, sl st in beg sc.

Rnd 7: Ch 1, sc in same st, (ch 6,* sc in next sc) 10 times, end last rep at *, sl st in beg sc.

Rnd 8: Ch 1, sc in same st, (7 sc in next ch-6 lp,* sc in next sc) 10 times, end last rep at *, sl st in beg sc. Fasten off.

gauge
finished motif = 3" in diameter

gauge
finished motif = 5½" x 5½"

heavy twine round

materials

- heavy sisal twine
- size H hook, or size required to obtain gauge

directions

Ch 6, sl st in beg ch to form a ring.

Rnd 1: Ch 3, 2 dc in ring, ch 1, (3 dc in ring, ch 1) 5 times, sl st in third ch in beg ch-3.

Rnd 2: Ch 3, dc in next 2 dc, (ch 3, 3 dc in next sp) 3 times, ch 3, dc in next 3 dc, rep bet ( ), ch 3, sl st in third ch of beg ch-3.

Rnd 3: Ch 1, sc in same st, sc in next 2 sts, (5 sc in next sp,* sc in next 3 sts) 8 times, end last rep at *, sl st in beg sc.

Rnd 4: [Ch 3, sk next st, sl st in next st, (ch 3, sk next 2 sts, sl st in next st) 2 times], rep bet [ ] around, end sl st in beg sl st. Fasten off.

byzantine cross block

materials
- ⅛"-wide silk ribbon
- size E hook, or size required to obtain gauge

directions

Ch 4, sl st in beg ch to form a ring.

Rnd 1: Ch 1, sc in center of ring, (ch 3,* sc in center of ring) 4 times, end last rep at *, sl st in beg sc.

Rnd 2: [Ch 5, sc in third ch from hk, sc in ea of next 2 ch, sl st in next sc bet ch-3 lps of Rnd 1, (ch 3, sl st in next sc of lp) 3 times, sl st in next sc bet ch-3 lps of Rnd 1], rep bet [ ] 3 times, sl st in first ch of beg ch-5. Fasten off.

gauge
finished motif = 2½" in diameter

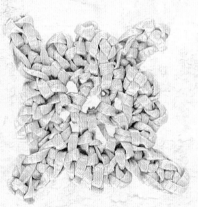

gauge
finished block = 2½" x 2½" at widest point

2-color flower

materials
- dk weight cotton yarn in color A
- dk weight cotton yarn in color B
- size F hook, or size required to obtain gauge

directions

Using col A, ch 4, sl st in beg ch to form a ring.

Rnd 1: (Ch 6, sl st in center of ring (petal made)) 8 times, sl st in beg ch. Fasten off.

Rnd 2: Using col B, join with sl st in center of ring bet any 2 petals, (ch 8, sl st in ring bet next 2 petals) 7 times, sl st in beg sl st. Fasten off.

designer block

materials
- acrylic/viscose yarn
- size E hook, or size required to obtain gauge

special stitches
2 dc cl

3 dc cl

directions
Ch 4, sl st in beg ch to form a ring.

Rnd 1: Ch 3, 2 dc in ring, (ch 3, 3 dc in ring) 5 times, ch 3, sl st in third ch of beg ch-3.

Rnd 2: Ch 3, 2 dc cl in ring, ch 2, 3 dc cl in ring, ch 2, [(3 dc cl, ch 2, 3 dc cl, ch 2, 3 dc cl) in next sp, ch 2], rep bet [ ] 5 times, 2 dc cl in same sp as beg, ch 2, sl st in third ch of beg ch-3.

Rnd 3: Ch 1, sc in same st, (ch 5, sc in next sp bet 3 dc cl groups,* ch 5, sc in top of center cl of next 3 dc cl group) 6 times, end last rep at *, ch 3, dc in beg sc.

Rnd 4: [Ch 5, sc in next lp, (ch 1, tr) 5 times in next sc, ch 1, sc in next lp], rep bet [ ] 5 times, except end last rep with sl st in top of closing dc of Rnd 3. Fasten off.

gauge
finished motif = 4½" in diameter

small solid block

materials

• lightweight silk yarn
• size D hook, or size required to obtain gauge

gauge

finished block = 1⅞" x 1⅞"

directions

Ch 12, sl st in beg ch to form a ring.

Rnd 1: Ch 3, 2 dc in ring, (ch 5, 3 dc) in ring 3 times, ch 5, sl st in third ch of beg ch-3.

Rnd 2: Ch 1, sc in same st, sc in next 2 dc, (5 sc in next ch-5 sp,* sc in next 3 dc) 4 times, end last rep at *, sl st in beg sc. Fasten off.

multicolor block

materials

• lightweight silk yarn
• size D hook, or size required to obtain gauge

directions

Ch 12, sl st in beg ch to form a ring.

Rnd 1: Ch 3, 2 dc in ring, (ch 5, 3 dc) in ring 3 times, ch 5, sl st in third ch of beg ch-3.

Rnd 2: Ch 1, sc in same st, sc in next 2 dc, (5 sc in next ch-5 sp,* sc in next 3 dc) 4 times, end last rep at *, sl st in beg sc.

Rnd 3: Ch 1, sc in ea sc around sl st in beg sc. Fasten off.

gauge

finished block = 2⅛" x 2⅛"

variegated lace triangle

materials
- lightweight bamboo yarn
- size D hook, or size required to obtain gauge

directions

Ch 8, sl st in beg ch to form a ring.

Rnd 1: Ch 1, 12 sc in ring, sl st in beg sc.

Rnd 2: Ch 8, sk next sc, dc in next sc, (ch 10, sk next sc,* dc in next sc, ch 5, sk next sc, dc in next sc) 3 times, end last rep at *, sl st in third ch of beg ch-8, sl st in next sp.

Rnd 3: Ch 3, 3 dc in same sp, [(4 dc, ch 7, 4 dc) in next ch-10 lp,* 4 dc in next sp], rep bet [ ] 3 times, end last rep at *, sl st in third ch of beg ch-3, sl st in next dc.

Rnd 4: Ch 1, sc in same st, ch 3, sk next 3 dc, dc in next dc, [ch 3, (4 dc, ch 3, 4 dc) in next ch-7 lp, ch 3, sk next dc, dc in next dc, ch 3, sk next 3 dc,* sc in next dc, ch 3, sk next 3 sts, dc in next dc], rep bet [ ] 2 times, end last rep at *, sl st in beg sc.

Rnd 5: Ch 1, sc in same st, (ch 5, sc in same st, 3 sc in next sp, sc in next dc, 3 sc in next sp, sc in ea of next 4 dc, 3 sc in next sp, sc in ea of next 4 dc, 3 sc in next sp, sc in next dc, 3 sc in next sp,* sc in next sc) 3 times, end last rep at *, sl st in beg sc. Fasten off.

gauge
finished motif = 4½" each side

round ruffle

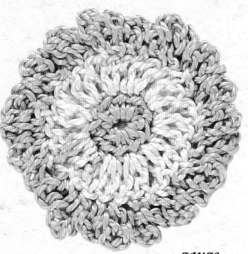

gauge
finished motif = 2½"
in diameter

materials

- #3 cotton crochet thread in color A
- #3 cotton crochet thread in color B
- size D hook, or size required to obtain gauge

directions
Using col A, ch 5, sl st in beg ch to form a ring.

Rnd 1: Ch 1, work 12 sc in ring, sl st in beg sc. Fasten off.

Rnd 2: Using col B, join with sl st in same sc as sl st, ch 3, dc in same st, (2 dc in next st) 11 times, sl st in third ch of beg ch-3. Fasten off.

Rnd 3: Using col A, join with sl st in same ch as sl st, work rnd in back lp only. Ch 1, sc in same st (ch 4, sc in next st) 23 times, end ch 4, sl st in beg sc. Fasten off.

delicate round

materials

- #10 cotton crochet thread in color A
- #10 cotton crochet thread in color B
- size D hook, or size required to obtain gauge

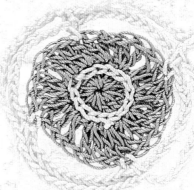

gauge
finished block = 2" x 2"

directions
Using col A, ch 4, sl st in beg ch to form a ring.

Rnd 1: Ch 2, 11 hdc in ring, sl st in second ch of beg ch-2.

Rnd 2: Ch 3, dc in same st, (2 dc in next st) 11 times, sl st in third ch of beg ch-3. (24 sts) Fasten off.

Rnd 3: Using col B, join with sl st bet any 2 dc, ch 1, sc in same st, (ch 12, sk 6 sts,* sc bet next 2 sts) 4 times, end last rep at *, sl st in beg sc.

Rnd 4: Ch 1, sc in same st, (ch 14,* sc in next sc) 4 times, end last rep at *, sl st in beg sc. Fasten off.

Rnd 5: *Note: This rnd will look like a ch st covering sts already worked.* Using col B, work around the post of hdc in Rnd 1, join with sl st in any st, with RS facing sl st on top of work in ea st around, end sl st in beg sl st. Fasten off and pl tail to WS of work.

bias tape block

materials
- cotton yarn
- size K hook, or size required to obtain gauge

directions
Ch 8, sl st in beg ch to form a ring.

Rnd 1: Ch 3, 2 dc in center of ring, (ch 2, 3 dc in ring) 3 times, end ch 2, sl st in third ch of beg ch-3.

Rnd 2: Ch 3, 3 dc in next dc, dc in next dc, [ch 1, (dc, ch 1, tr ch 1, dc) in next ch-2 sp, ch 1,* dc in next dc, 3 dc in next dc, dc in next dc], rep bet [ ] 3 times, end last rep at *, sl st in third ch of beg ch-3.

Rnd 3: Ch 3, [(dc around the post of next dc, dc in next dc) 2 times, dc around post of next dc, 2 dc in next ch-1 sp, ch 1 (corner) 2 dc in next ch-1 sp, dc around post of next dc,* dc in next dc], rep bet [ ] 3 times, end last rep at *, sl st in third ch of beg ch-3.

Rnd 4: Ch 1, sc in same st, [sc in ea st to corner, (sc, ch 1 sc) in ch-1 sp], rep bet [ ] 3 times, end sc in next 2 sts, sl st in third ch of beg ch-3. Fasten off.

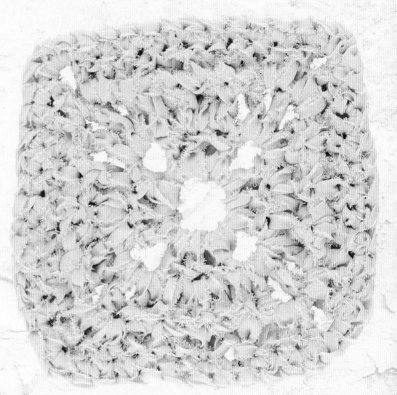

gauge
finished block = 7" x 7"

gauge
finished block = 4½" x 4½"

soft cotton block

materials
- size F hook, or size required to obtain gauge
- sport weight cotton yarn

directions
Ch 4, sl st in beg ch to form a ring.

Rnd 1: Ch 6, (3 dc in center of ring, ch 3) 3 times, 2 dc in ring, sl st in third ch of beg ch-6.

Rnd 2: Sl st in next sp, ch 6, dc in same sp, [dc in next st, 2 dc in next st, dc in next st,* (dc, ch 3, dc) in next sp], rep bet [ ] 3 times, end last rep at *, sl st in third ch of beg ch-6.

Rnd 3: Sl st in next sp, ch 6, dc in same sp, [(sk next st, dc in next st, dc in sk st) 3 times* (dc, ch 3, dc) in next sp], rep bet [ ] 3 times, end last rep at *, sl st in third ch of beg ch-6.

Rnd 4: Sl st in next sp, ch 6, dc in same sp [ch 1, (sk next st, dc in next st, dc in sk st) 4 times, ch 1* (dc, ch 3, dc) in next sp], rep bet [ ] 3 times, end last rep at *, sl st in third ch of beg ch-6, sl st in next 2 ch. Leave an 18" tail for sewing. Fasten off.

scallop block

materials

- fine-weight cotton crepe yarn
- size 1 steel hook, or size required to obtain gauge

directions

Ch 4, sl st in beg ch to form a ring.

Rnd 1: Ch 3, 15 dc in center of ring. (16 sts)

Rnd 2: Ch 3, dc in next 3 sts, (ch 5, dc in next 4 sts) 3 times, end ch 3, sl st in top of beg ch-3.

Rnd 3: Ch 3, dc in next 3 sts, [ch 1, (2 dc, ch 3, 2 dc) in ch-5 sp, ch 1,* dc in next 4 sts], rep bet [ ] 3 times, end last rep at *, sl st in top of beg ch-3.

Rnd 4: (Ch 3, 3 dc in same st, sk next 2 dc, sl st in next dc, ch 3, 3 dc in same st, sk next ch and next dc, sl st in next dc, ch 3, 3 dc in same st, sk next 2 ch, sl st in next dc, ch 3, 3 dc in same dc, sk next dc and ch, sl st in next dc) 4 times. (16 petals)

Rnd 5: Sl st in next 3 ch (to point of petal), ch 1, sc bet ch-3 and next dc, (ch 5, sc bet ch-3 and next dc) 2 times, [ch 7 (corner), sc bet ch 3 and next dc,* rep bet ( ) 3 times], rep bet [ ] 3 times, end last rep at *, ch 5, sl st in beg sc.

Rnd 6: Ch 1, sc in same st, (5 sc in next lp, sc in next sc) 2 times [(3 sc, ch 3, 3 sc) in corner sp, sc in next sc, rep bet ( ) 3 times], rep bet [ ] 3 times, end 5 sc in next lp, sl st in beg sc. Fasten off.

gauge

finished block = 4" x 4"

small variegated flower

gauge
finished motif =
1½" in diameter

materials
• #10 cotton crochet thread in color A
• #10 cotton crochet thread in color B
• size D hook, or size required to obtain gauge

directions
Using col A, ch 4, sl st in beg ch to form a ring.

Rnd 1: Ch 1, 8 sc in ring, sl st in beg sc. Fasten off.

Rnd 2: Using col B and working in front lp only, join with sl st in any sc, ch 1, sc in same st, (ch 3,* sc in next sc) 8 times, end last rep at *, sl st in beg sc.

Rnd 3: Work rnd in back lp only. Sl st in back lp of same st, ch 1, sc in same st, (ch 5,* sc in next sc) 8 times, end last rep at *, sl st in beg sc. Fasten off.

rainbow flower

materials
• #3 viscose crochet thread
• size D hook, or size required to obtain gauge

directions
Ch 9, sl st in beg ch to form a ring.

Rnd 1: Ch 1, 13 sc in center of ring, sl st in beg sc.

Rnd 2: Ch 3, 2 dc in same st, ch 3, (3 dc in next st, ch 3) 12 times, sl st in third ch of beg ch-3.

Rnd 3: Ch 1, (sc in ea of next 3 dc, 3 sc in ch-3 sp) 13 times, sl st in beg sc. Fasten off.

gauge
finished motif = 2¼" in diameter

spiral rainbow flower

materials
- #3 viscose crochet thread
- size D hook, or size required to obtain gauge

directions

Ch 9, sl st in beg ch to form a ring.

Rnd 1: Ch 1, work 12 sc in center of ring, sl st in beg sc.

Rnd 2: Ch 3, 3 dc in same st, (sk next st, ch 3, 4 dc in next st) 5 times, dc in third ch of beg ch-3.

Rnd 3: Ch 3, 3 dc in next sp, (ch 10, 4 dc in next sp) 5 times, ch 10, sl st in third ch of beg ch-3.

Rnd 4: Ch 1, sc in same st, sc in next 3 dc, (9 sc in next lp,* sc in next 4 dc) 6 times, end last rep at *, sl st in beg sc.

Rnd 5: Ch 1, sc in same st, sc in next 7 sc, [(hdc, 3 dc, ch 1, hdc) in next st, sc in next 12 sc], rep bet [ ] 5 times, sc in next 4 sc, sl st in beg sc. Fasten off.

gauge
finished motif = 4½" in diameter at widest point

pansy motif

gauge

finished motif =
3" x 3½"

materials

• cotton sport weight yarn

• size F hook, or size required to obtain gauge

directions

Ch 4, sl st in beg ch to form a ring.

Rnd 1: Ch 1, (sc in ring, ch 3) 4 times, sl st in beg sc.

Rnd 2: [(Sc, ch 3, 4 dc, ch 3, sc) in next ch-3 lp,] 4
times, sl st to beg sc.

Rnd 3: Ch 6, [sc in next ch-3 lp, ch 5, sk next dc, sc in
next dc, (ch 5, sc in next dc) 2 times, ch 5, sc in next ch-
3 lp], ch 3, sc around post of next sc of Rnd 1, ch 3, rep
bet [ ], end ch 6, sl st bet next 2 sc. Fasten off.

baby block

gauge

finished block =
2" x 2"

materials

• acrylic baby yarn in color A

• acrylic/orlon yarn in color B

• size G hook, or size required to obtain gauge

directions

Using col B, ch 3, sl st in beg ch to form a ring.

Rnd 1: Ch 2, hdc in ring, ch 1, (2 hdc in ring, ch 1)
3 times, sl st in second ch of beg ch-2. Fasten off.

Rnd 2: Using col A, join with sl st in any ch-1 sp, ch 2,
hdc in same ch-1 sp, (ch 2, 2 hdc in same ch-1 sp, ch
1,* 2 hdc in next ch-1 sp), rep bet ( ) 3 times, end last
rep at *, sl st into second ch of beg ch-2.

Rnd 3: Using col B, join with sl st in any ch-2 sp, ch 1, 2
sc in same ch-2 sp, [sc in ea of next 2 hdc sts, sc in ch-1
sp, sc in ea of next 2 hdc sts,* 3 sc in corner ch-2 sp], rep
bet [ ] 3 times, end last rep at *, sl st in beg ch-1.
Fasten off.

cotton flower & square

materials

- lightweight cotton yarn in color A
- lightweight cotton yarn in color B
- lightweight cotton yarn in color C
- lightweight cotton yarn in color D
- size E hook, or size required to obtain gauge

directions

Flower Motif: Using col A, ch 4, sl st in beg ch to form a ring.

Rnd 1: (Ch 3, dc in ring, ch 3, sl st in ring,) 4 times. Fasten off. (4 petals)

Rnd 2: Using col B, join yarn with [sc in center of ring bet 2 petals, ch 3, sk next ch, sc in back lp only of next dc, ch 3, sk next ch, sc in back lp only of next ch, ch 3) 4 times, sl st in beg sc. Fasten off.

Square: Using col A, ch 4, sl st in beg ch to form a ring.

Rnd 1: (Ch 3, dc in ring, ch 3, sl st in ring) 4 times. Fasten off. (4 petals)

Rnd 2: Using col B, join with (sc in center of ring bet 2 petals, ch 3, sk next ch, sc in back lp only of next dc, ch 3, sk next ch, sc in back lp only of next ch, ch 3] 4 times, sl st in beg sc. Fasten off.

Rnd 3: *Note: Work in back lp only, except when working around post sts.* Using col C, join with (sc, ch 1, sc) in sc at point of next petal (corner st) [ch 1, sk next st, sc in next ch, ch 1, sk next st, sc in next sc, dc around post of next sc of rnd below, sk next 3 ch, sc in next sc, ch 1, sk next st, sc in next ch, ch 1,* (sc, ch 1, sc) in next corner

st], rep bet [ ] 3 times, end last rep at *, sl st in back lp only of corner ch-1 st.

Rnd 4: Ch 1, (sc, ch 1, sc) in same st, sk next sc, [(ch 1, sc in next sc) 2 times, ch 1 sk next dc post st, (sc in next sc, ch 1) 2 times,* (sc, ch 1, sc) in next corner ch-1 sp], rep bet [ ] 3 times, end last rep at *, sl st in beg sc. Fasten off.

Rnd 5: Using col D, join with sc in first sc past any corner section (ch 1, sc in next sc) 5 times, [ch 1, (dc, ch 1, dc) in corner ch-1 sp of Rnd 2, (ch 1,* sc in next sc) 6 times] rep bet [ ] 3 times, end last rep at *, sl st in beg sc. Fasten off.

gauge
finished block = 3½" x 3½"

gauge
finished motif = 1½" x 1½"

fuzzy eyelash block

gauge
finished block = 5" x 5"

materials

- polyester eyelash yarn in color B
- size F hook, or size required to obtain gauge
- sport weight cotton yarn in color A

directions

Using col A, ch 4, sl st in beg ch to form a ring.

Rnd 1: Ch 6, (3 dc in center of ring, ch 3) 3 times, 2 dc in ring, sl st in third ch of beg ch-6.

Rnd 2: Sl st in next 2 ch, ch 6, 3 dc in same sp, (ch 1, 3 dc, ch 3, 3 dc in next sp) 3 times, 2 dc in same sp as beg, sl st in third ch of beg ch-6.

Rnd 3: Sl st in next 2 ch, ch 6, 3 dc in same sp, [ch 1, 3 dc in next ch-1 sp, ch 1* (3 dc, ch 3, 3 dc) in same st], rep bet [ ] 3 times, end last rep at *, 2 dc in same sp as beg, sl st in third ch of beg ch-6.

Rnd 4: Sl st in next 2 ch, ch 6, 3 dc in same sp, [(ch 1, 3 dc in next ch-1 sp) 2 times, ch 1* (3 dc, ch 3, 3 dc) in next ch-3 corner sp], rep bet [ ] 4 times, end last rep at *, 2 dc in same sp as beg, sl st in third ch of beg ch-6. Leave a tail for sewing. Fasten off.

Trim:

Rnd 1: Using col B and working around top of Rnd 1 of block, sc in any corner sp before 3-dc section, (ch 3, sc in next corner sp, ch 3, sc in same corner sp beyond 6-dc section of Rnd 2) 4 times.

Rnd 2: [Ch 3, sc in next ch-1 sp of Rnd 2 of block (before 3-dc section), ch 3, sc in same ch-1 sp (beyond 3-dc section), ch 3, sc in corner ch-3 sp, after first 3-dc of corner section of Rnd 1], rep bet [ ] around, sl st in beg st.

snuggly soft block

materials
- dk weight acrylic blend yarn
- size F hook, or size required to obtain gauge

gauge
finished block = 4" x 4"

special stitches
2 dc cl

3 dc cl

directions
Ch 4, sl st in beg ch to form a ring.

Rnd 1: Ch 3, work 2 dc cl in ring, (ch 2, work 3 dc cl in ring) 7 times, end dc in third ch of beg ch-3.

Rnd 2: Ch 3, work 2 dc cl in next ch-2 sp, ch 2, work a 3 dc cl in same sp, [ch 2, work 3 dc cl in next sp, ch 2,* (3 dc cl, ch 2, 3 dc cl) in next sp], rep bet [ ] 4 times, end last rep at *, sc in beg ch-3.

Rnd 3: [(Ch 1, dc) 5 times in next ch-2 sp, ch 1, sc in next sp, ch 3, sc in next sp], rep bet [ ] 3 times, sl st in closing sc of Rnd 2. Fasten off.

cluster block

materials

- size F hook, or size required to obtain gauge
- sport weight cotton yarn in color A
- sport weight cotton yarn in color B

directions

Using col A, ch 4, sl st in beg ch to form a ring.

Rnd 1: Ch 6, [(dc, ch 1, 3 dc cl, ch 1* dc) in center of ring, ch 3], rep bet [ ] 3 times, end last rep at *, sl st in third ch of beg ch-6. Fasten off.

Rnd 2: Using col B, join with sl st in next sp (corner), ch 6, dc in same sp, [(ch 1, 3 dc cl in next ch-1 sp), 2 times, ch 1* (dc, ch 3, dc) in next ch-3 corner sp], rep bet [ ] 3 times, end last rep at *, sl st in third ch of beg ch-6. Fasten off.

Rnd 3: Using col A, join with sl st in next sp (corner), ch 6, dc in same sp, [(ch 1, 3 dc cl in next ch-1 sp) 3 times, ch 1* (dc, ch 3, dc) in next ch-3 sp], rep bet [ ] 3 times, end last rep at *, sl st in third ch of beg ch-6. Fasten off.

Rnd 4: Using col B, join with sl st in next sp (corner), ch 4, 3 dc cl, ch 3, 3 dc cl, ch 1 dc in same corner sp [(ch 1, dc in next ch-1 sp) 4 times, ch 1* (dc, ch 1, 3 dc cl, ch 3, 3 dc cl, ch 1, dc) in next corner sp], rep bet [ ] 3 times, end last rep at *, sl st in third ch of beg ch-4, sl st in next 3 sts to center of next corner sp. Leave a tail for sewing. Fasten off.

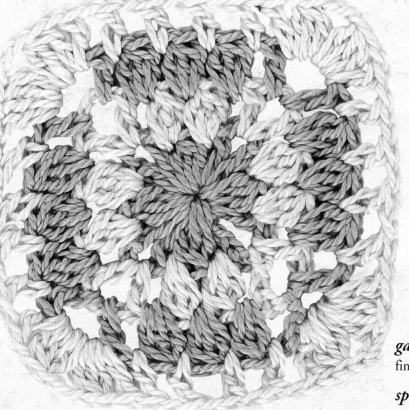

gauge
finished block = 5" x 5"

special stitches
3 dc cl

64

outside-in block

gauge
finished block =
approx. 4¼" x 4¼"

materials

- cotton yarn
- size H hook, or size required to obtain gauge

directions

Note: This block is made from the outside in.

Ch 72, sl st into beg ch making a ring. Be certain not to twist the chain when you connect it.

Rnd 1: [(Corner begins) Ch 3, (sk 1 ch, dc in next ch without working off last 2 lps) 5 times, then yo, pl lp thr all (6) lps on hk. Ch 1 and tighten (making eye), ch 2, sk 1 ch and sl st in next ch (corner finished). (Side shell begins) Sk 2 ch, 6 dc in next ch, sk 2 ch, sl st in next ch (side shell finished)], rep bet [ ] 3 times, sl st in first ch of beg ch-3.

Rnd 2: Ch 1, turn to WS, working in last sts just made sl st in next 3 st, sl st in bet third and fourth dc of side shell, turn to RS. Ch 3, 2 dc in same sp bet third and fourth dc of side shell, 1 dc in eye where the corner dc come tog, (6 dc bet third and fourth dc of next side shell, 1 dc in eye where the corner dc come tog) 3 times, end with 3 dc bet third and fourth dc of next side shell (starting place), sl st into third ch of beg ch-3. Fasten off.

lacy baby
afghan block

materials

- acrylic baby yarn
- size G hook, or size required to obtain gauge (a size G 10" long afghan hook may be more convenient)

directions

Ch 17.

Rows 1–13: Work afghan st for 13 rows (16 sts).

Rnd 1 (Block Edging): Ch 4, 2 dc at base of ch-4, (sk 2 st, 2 dc in next st) 4 times, ch 1 (block top completed). In corner st, work (2 dc, ch 1, 2 dc, ch 1, 2 dc, ch 1). Continue working down side of block as follows: sk 2 st, 2 dc in next st, ch 1, sk 1 st, 2 dc in next st, ch 1, sk 2 st, 2 dc in next st, ch 1, sk 1 st, 2 dc, ch 1 (block side completed). Work corner st as before. Work along bottom of block in the same manner as top of block, then ch 1 and work corner st as before. Continue to work the (last) side of the block in same manner as other side was worked to corner, in same corner as beg work: ch 1, 2 dc, ch 1, 1 dc, sl st in third ch of beg ch-4, sl st in next ch-1 sp.

Rnd 2 (Picots): Ch 1, sc in same sp, [ch 4, sl st in third ch from hk, ch 1, sk 2 dc, sc in next ch-1 sp bet groups of dc (1 picot completed)]. Rep bet [ ] around entire block, end with sl st into beg sc. Fasten off.

gauge

finished block = 5½" x 5½"

special stitches

afghan st

gauge
finished block = 5½" x 5½"

special stitches
afghan st

Design in Center of Block: *Note: Many different shapes can be made, such as flower, heart, star, fish, bunny face, hugs and kisses (X O), etc. The model blocks show a pink flower (on pink square), and a white star (on blue square). The shape of the design is made with ch sts, which are secured to the body of the block with sl st. The ch sts are relief sts floating on top of block.* With RS facing, join trim col with sl st at appropriate beg place on front of block. Work a few ch sts, according to desired shape, and anchor to front of block with sl st. Continue working until shape is made. End by sl st into beg ch or appropriate ending place. Fasten off.

Additional Trim: If desired, ribbon may be interwoven thr the dc in Rnd 1 of the block edging, and tied in a bow.

varied color blocks

materials

- dk weight cotton yarn in color A
- dk weight cotton yarn in color B
- dk weight cotton yarn in color C
- size F hook, or size required to obtain gauge

directions

Variation 1: Using col A, ch 4, sl st in beg ch to form a ring.

Rnd 1: Ch 4, 2 tr in center of ring, ch 2, sc in ring, ch 2, 3 tr in ring, ch 3, 3 tr in ring, ch 2, sc in ring, ch 2, 3 tr in ring, ch 3, sl st in fourth ch of beg ch-4. Fasten off.

Rnd 2: Using col B, join in same st with sl st, ch 1, sc in same st [(ch 3, sc in next tr) 2 times, ch 3, sc in next ch-3 sp, tr around post of next sc, sc in next ch-3 sp, (ch 3, sc in next tr) 3 times, tr around the posts of same tr and next tr together,* sc in second of the tr sts of Rnd 1 of which the post was just worked], rep bet [ ], end rep at *, sl st in beg sc. Fasten off.

Variation 2: Work Rnd 1 with col B, work Rnd 2 with col C.

Variation 3: Work Rnd 1 with col C, work Rnd 2 with col A.

Other Variations: Change colors of Rnd 1 and Rnd 2 as desired.

gauge

finished block = 2½" x 3"

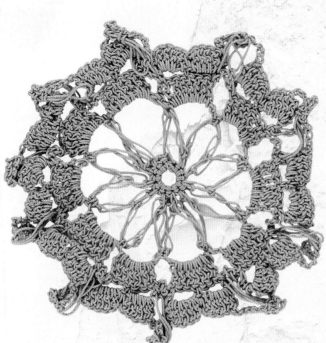

gauge
finished motif = 6" in diameter at widest point

special stitches
lovers' lp

lovers' loop round

materials
- #10 cotton crochet thread
- size 6 hook, or size required to obtain gauge

directions
Ch 7, sl st in beg ch to form a ring.

Rnd 1: Ch 1, 10 sc in center of ring, sl st in beg sc.

Rnd 2: Ch 1, sc in same st, make lovers' lp as follows: [(pl up lp 1", ch 1) 2 times,* sc in next sc in ring], rep bet [ ] 9 times, end last rep at *, sl st in beg sc. Fasten off.

Rnd 3: Join with sc in top of any lp, (ch 8,* sc in next lp) 10 times, end last rep at *, sl st in beg sc.

Rnd 4: Sl st in next ch-8 sp, ch 3, 6 dc in same sp, (ch 5, 7 dc in next sp) 9 times, ch 5, sl st in third ch of beg ch-3.

Rnd 5: Ch 1, sc in same st, [(ch 5, sk next 2 dc, sc in next st) 2 times, make a lovers' lp, sk next ch-5 lp,* sc in next dc], rep bet [ ] 9 times, end last rep at *, sl st in beg sc.

Rnd 6: Ch 3, (3 dc, hdc) in next ch-5 sp, [sc in next sc, (hdc, 4 dc) in next sp, ch 5, (sc, ch 5, sc) in center ch of next lovers' lp, ch 5,* (4 dc, hdc) in next sp] rep bet [ ] 9 times, end last rep at *, sl st in third ch of beg ch-3. Fasten off.

loops & arches

materials

- #10 cotton crochet thread
- size 6 hook, or size required to obtain gauge

directions

Ch 8, sl st in beg ch to form a ring.

Rnd 1: Ch 1, 16 sc in center of ring, sl st in beg sc.

Rnd 2: Ch 3, dc in next st, (ch 2, dc in next 4 sts) 3 times, ch 2, dc in next 2 sts, sl st in third ch of beg ch-3.

Rnd 3: Ch 4, tr in same st, [(ch 5, 2 tr) in next ch-2 sp, ch 5,* sk next 2 dc, 2 tr bet second and third dc of next group], rep bet [ ] 3 times, end last rep at *, sl st in fourth ch of beg ch-4, sl st in next dc and in next sp.

Rnd 4: Ch 3, (3 dc, ch 1, 4 dc) in same sp, [ch 1, (4 dc, ch 1, 4 dc) in next ch-5 sp], rep bet [ ] 7 times, ch 1, sl st in third ch of beg ch-3, sl st in next 3 sts, sl st in next ch-1 sp.

Rnd 5: Ch 3, 9 dc in same sp, (sc in next ch-1 sp, 10 dc in next ch-1 sp) 7 times, sc in next ch-1 sp, sl st in third ch of beg ch-3.

Rnd 6: Ch 1, sc in same sp, (ch 4, sc in next dc) around, sl st in beg sc. Fasten off.

gauge
finished motif = 4½" diameter at widest point

open block

materials

- #10 cotton crochet thread
- size 6 steel hook, or size required to obtain gauge

directions

Ch 10, sl st in beg ch to form a ring.

Rnd 1: Ch 1, 12 sc in center of ring, sl st in beg sc.

Rnd 2: Ch 3, dc in same st, 2 dc in ea of next 2 sts, (ch 2, 2 dc in ea of next 3 sts) 3 times, ch 2, sl st in third ch of beg ch-3.

Rnd 3: Ch 6, sk next 2 dc, dc in next dc, [ch 3, sk next dc, dc in next dc, ch 10, sk next ch-2,* dc in next dc, ch 3, sk next 2 dc, dc in next dc], rep bet [ ] 3 times, end last rep at *, sl st in third ch of beg ch-6.

Rnd 4: Ch 6, dc in next dc, ch 3, dc in next dc, [(5 dc, ch 8, 5 dc) in next ch-10 sp,* dc in next dc, (ch 3, dc in next dc) 2 times], rep bet [ ] 3 times, end last rep at *, sl st in third ch of beg ch-6, sl st in next 3 ch, sl st in next dc.

Rnd 5: [Ch 12, sk across sts to next ch-8 sp, 10 tr in this ch-8 sp, ch 12, sk across 6 dc and 3 ch, sl st in next dc], rep bet [ ] 3 times.

Rnd 6: [(Sc, ch 4 in next ch-12 lp) 8 times, sc in same lp, sc in next 5 tr, ch 5, sc in next 5 tr, (sc, ch 4 in next ch-12 lp) 8 times], rep bet [ ] 3 times, end sl st in beg sc. Fasten off.

gauge
finished motif = 5" x 5"

patchwork pocket

materials

- #3 cotton crochet thread in color C
- cotton worsted weight yarn in color A
- cotton worsted weight yarn in color B
- size F hook, or size required to obtain gauge

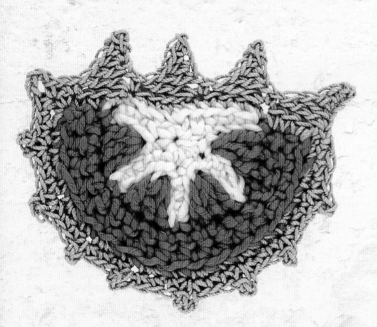

gauge
finished motif = 4¾" x 4"

directions

Using col A, ch 4, sl st in beg ch to form a ring.

Rnd 1: Ch 1, sc in ring, (ch 4, sc in second ch from hk, sc in ea of next 2 ch,* sc in ring) 5 times, end last rep at *, sl st in beg sc. Fasten off. Position spokes so there is a straight edge bet 2 spokes.

Note: Work next 3 rows in back lp only.

Rnd 2: Using col B, join with sl st in tip of spoke at RS of motif, ch 1, sc in same place, (3 dc in next sc (bet spokes) in Rnd 1, sc in tip of next spoke) 4 times. Turn.

Rnd 3: Ch 1, sc in same st, sc in ea of next 16 sts, = 17 sts. Turn.

Rnd 4: Ch 1, 2 sc in same st, sc in ea of next 15 sts, 2 sc in last st, = 19 sts. Fasten off.

Rnd 5: With RS facing, work around entire motif. Using col C, join with sl st in top of last sc just worked in Row 4, [ch 1, sc, ch 1, sc] in same st (corner), sc in side of next 3 rows of col B, 11 sc across center sts worked in col A, sc in side of next 3 rows of col B across flat side of motif, [sc, ch 1, sc] in same st (corner) [sc in next sc, 2 sc in next st] 8 times, sc in next sc, sl st in beg sc, sl st in ch-1 sp, sl st in ea of next 2 scs.

Rnd 6: Ch 1, sc in same sc (base st), ch 5, sc in second ch from hk, sc in third ch, hdc in fourth ch, dc in fifth ch, tr in same sc as beg sc (base st), [sk next 3 sc of Rnd 5, sc in next sc (base st) ch 5, sc in second ch from hk, sc in third ch, hdc in fourth ch, dc in fifth ch, tr in same st in Rnd 5 (base st)] 3 times, sk next 3 sc, sc in ea of next 2 sc, [sc, ch 3, sc] in ch-1 corner sp, [sc in next 2 sc, (sc, ch 3, sc) in next st], rep bet [ ] 8 times, sc in next sc to corner, sl st in beg sc. Fasten off.

cotton string round

materials

- #3 cotton yarn
- size E hook, or size required to obtain gauge

directions

Ch 5, sl st in beg ch to form a ring.

Rnd 1: (Ch 1, sc in ring) 5 times, do not join.

Rnd 2: *Note: Continue as a spiral in Rnds 2–6, mark last sc with a safety pin and move it up at completion of ea rnd* (Ch 3, sc in next sc) 5 times.

Rnds 3–4: (Ch 3, sk next st, sc in next st) around. (20 lps at end of Rnd 4)

Rnd 5: (Ch 5, sc in next ch-3 lp) 20 times.

Rnd 6: (Ch 2, sc in next ch-5 lp) 20 times, sl st in next sc. Remove marker pin, sl st in next ch-2 sp.

Rnd 7: *Note: Now work in completed rnds.* Ch 3, 2 dc in same sp, (ch 2, 3 dc in next sp) 20 times, ch 2, sl st in third ch of beg ch-3 (21 dc groups).

Rnd 8: Ch 1, [(sc bet next 2 dcs) 2 times, 2 sc in next ch-2 sp] 21 times, sl st in beg sc. Fasten off.

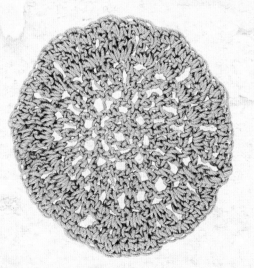

gauge
finished motif = 4½" in diameter

cotton string loops & arches

gauge
finished motif = 3½" in diameter

materials

- #3 cotton yarn
- size E hook, or size required to obtain gauge

directions

Ch 5, sl st in beg ch to form a ring.

Rnd 1: Ch 1, (sc in ring) 8 times, sl st in beg sc.

Rnd 2: Ch 1, sc in same st, (ch 3, sk next st,* sc in next st) 4 times, end last rep at *, sl st in beg sc.

Rnd 3: Ch 1, sc in same st (ch 6, sk next 3 ch,* sc in next sc) 4 times, end last rep at *, sl st in beg sc.

Rnd 4: Ch 1, sc in same st, (ch 6, sc in next ch-6 lp, ch 6,* sc in next sc) 4 times, end last rep at *, sl st in beg sc.

Rnd 5: Ch 1, sc in same st, (ch 8,* sc in next sc) 8 times, end last rep at *, sl st in beg sc.

Rnd 6: Ch 1, sc in same st, (ch 4, sc in same st, 8 sc in next ch-8 lp,* sc in next sc) 8 times, end last rep at *, sl st in beg sc. Fasten off.

silky block

materials
- acrylic/nylon sport weight yarn in color A
- acrylic/nylon sport weight yarn in color B
- acrylic/nylon sport weight yarn in color C
- size F hook, or size required to obtain gauge

directions
Using col B, ch 4, sl st in beg ch to form a ring.

Rnd 1: Ch 3, 2 dc in center of ring, ch 1, (3 dc in ring, ch 1) 3 times, sl st in third ch of beg ch-3. Fasten off.

Rnd 2: Using col A, join with sl st in any ch-1 sp, ch 3, (2 dc, ch 1, 3 dc) in same sp (corner), ch 1, [(3 dc, ch 1 3 dc) in next sp, ch 1], rep bet [ ] 2 times, sl st in third ch of beg ch-3. Fasten off.

Rnd 3: Using col C, join with sl st in any corner ch-1 sp, ch 3, (2 dc, ch 1, 3 dc) in same sp, [(ch 1, 3 dc in next sp, ch 1,* 3 dc, ch 1, 3 dc) in next corner ch-1 sp], rep bet [ ] 3 times, end last rep at *, sl st in third ch of beg ch-3. Fasten off.

Rnd 4: Using col A, join with sl st in any corner ch-1 sp, ch 1, [(sc, ch 1 sc) in corner sp, sc in next 11 sts] 4 times, sl st in beg sc, sl st in next ch-1 sp.

Rnd 5: Ch 8, dc in same sp, [(ch 2, sk next 2 sts, dc in next st) 2 times, ch 2, sk next st, dc in next st, rep bet ( ) once, ch 2, sk next 2 sts,* (dc, ch 5, dc) in next corner ch-1 sp], rep bet [ ] 3 times, end last rep at *, sl st in third ch of beg ch-8. Fasten off.

gauge
finished block = 4"

special stitches
lp st

rounded heart motif

materials

- #3 cotton crochet thread
- size D hook, or size required to obtain gauge
- tapestry needle

gauge

finished motif = 2" x 2"

directions

Ch 5, sl st in beg ch to form a ring.

Rnd 1: Ch 1, (sc in ring, ch 4) 6 times, sl st in beg sc.

Rnd 2: Ch 1, sc in same st, (4 sc in next lp,* sc in next sc) 6 times, end last rep at *, sl st in beg sc.

Rnds 3–4: Ch 1, sc in same st, sc in ea st around (30 sts completed). Cut thread, leaving a 4" tail.

Finishing: Thread tapestry needle with tail, sew 3 running sts toward center of motif, (directly under beg sc of Rnd 4) over 1 rnd and under the next to center ring. Pl tightly and secure. Fasten off.

small string flower

gauge

finished motif = 1" in diameter

materials

- #3 cotton crochet thread
- size D hook, or size required to obtain gauge

directions

Ch 5, sl st in beg ch to form a ring.

Rnd 1: Ch 1, (sc, ch 3 in ring) 5 times, sl st in beg sc. Fasten off.

twine rectangle

materials
• heavy-weight sisal twine
• size H hk, or size required to obtain gauge

gauge
finished block = 1½" x 4½"

special stitches
3 dc cl

directions
Ch 7, turn.

Row 1: Ch 3, dc in ea st across, turn.

Row 2: Ch 1, sc in same st, sc in ea st across, turn.

Row 3: Ch 3, sk next st, 3 dc in next st (shell), sk next st, dc in last st, turn.

Row 4: Rep Row 2.

Row 5: Ch 4, work 3 dc cl over next 3 sts, ch 1, dc in last st, turn.

Row 6: Rep Row 2.

Row 7: Rep Row 1. Fasten off.

gauge
finished motif = 2" in diameter

mohair flower

materials
• mohair yarn
• size E hook, or size required to obtain gauge
• tapestry needle

directions
Ch 6, sl st in beg ch to form a ring.

Rnd 1: Ch 1, 12 sc in ring, sl st in beg sc.

Rnd 2: Ch 1, sc in same st, [(hdc, dc, 2 tr, dc, hdc) in next st,* sc in next st], rep bet [ ] 6 times, end last rep at *, sl st in beg sc. Fasten off.

beaded block

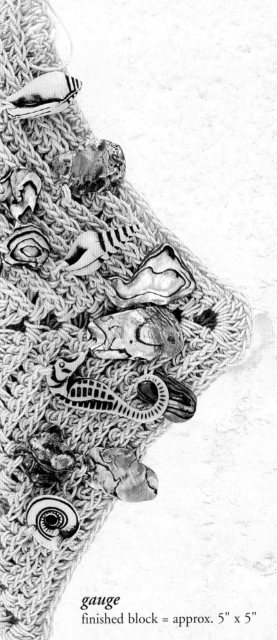

materials
- assorted beads
- cotton crochet thread
- size 6 steel hook, or size required to obtain gauge

directions
Note: Beads are placed randomly as desired on only half the block (triangular-shaped half). At the point a bead is to be strung, finish the dc, draw the thread lp thru the bead and continue crochet as before. A needle-threader or small-eyed needle and thread may be useful when drawing the thread thr the bead.

Ch 4, sl st in beg ch, making a ring.

Rnd 1: Ch 3, 3 dc in ring, ch 3, [4 dc in ring, ch 3] 3 times, sl st in third ch of beg ch-3, turn, sl st into ch-3 (corner) sp, turn.

Rnds 2–7: Ch 3, dc in same ch-3 sp, [bpdc around ea dc st along the side of the block, (2 dc, ch 3,* 2 dc) in ch-3 corner sp], rep bet [ ] 3 times, end last rep at *, sl st in third ch of beg ch-3, turn, sl st into ch-3 sp, turn.

Rnd 8: Ch 3, dc in same ch-3 sp, [bpdc around ea dc st along the side of the block, 7 dc in corner ch-3 sp], rep bet [ ] 3 times, end last rep with just 5 dc in corner ch-3 sp, sl st in third ch of beg ch-3. Fasten off.

gauge
finished block = approx. 5" x 5"

special stitches
bpdc

chapter 2:
embellishments

Transforming an item of clothing is fun and easy with beautiful granny squares. Pull out those old skirts, blouses, dresses—all those things you've tired of or that need a little embellishing—and give them a new updated look with crochet.

trefoil motif

Here is an example of "rescued" granny squares used to embellish clothing. This fun white peasant skirt was adapted from an old tablecloth that had both crochet and embroidery panels in it. The crochet panels were actually worked around the cloth panels, including around the top and bottom of each panel. I separated it from itself carefully—a painful task when considering the amount of time the original artisan spent working on it!—and repaired the ends where needed. Other than being stitched to the top and zipper back of the skirt, the horizontal panel was left free to hang down.

silk ribbon embellishments

This white wool jacket needed little enhancement. I chose to accent its darker cream colors by making simple ovals of old silk ribbon to stitch on the pockets. Old glass pearls were added to these ovals and also up at the notch in the collar to tie the pieces together.

materials
- ⅛"-wide silk knit ribbon yarn
- size E hook, or size required to obtain gauge

gauge
finished motif A = ½" x 2"
finished motif B = ½" x 2"

directions
Note: Make 2 Motifs A.

Motif A: Ch 12, sl st in beg ch to form a ring, turn.

Rnd 1: With WS facing, ch 1, sc in same st, make a "bobble" in next st as follows: (yo, insert hk in st, pl up 1 lp) 3 times, yo, pl yarn thr 7 lps on hk, ch 1, (sc in next st, bobble in next st) 2 times, sc in next 6 sts, sl st in beg sc. Turn.

Rnd 2: With RS facing, ch 5, sk next st, sc in next st, (ch 4, sk next st, sc in next st) 2 times, (ch 4, sk next bobble, sc in next st) 3 times, sl st in first ch of beg ch-5. Leave a tail for decoration. Fasten off.

Note: Make 2 Motifs B.

Motif B: *Note: Reverse shaping to have bobbles on opposite side.* Ch 12, sl st in beg ch to form a ring.

Rnd 1: Ch 1, sc in same st, sc in next 5 sts, (make a bobble in next st, sc in next st) 3 times, sl st in beg sc. Turn.

Rnd 2: Ch 5, sk next bobble, sc in next st, (ch 4, sk next bobble, sc in next st) 2 times, (ch 4, sk next st, sc in next st) 3 times, sl st to first ch of beg ch-5. Leave a tail for decoration. Fasten off.

delicate flower motifs

These flowers enhance a cool light tunic. I used sparkly gem accents to further embellish the beautiful motifs.

materials
- cotton crochet thread
- size 1 steel hook, or size required to obtain gauge

directions

Flower Motif A: Leave an 8" tail before beg for sewing. Ch 4, sl st in beg ch to form a ring, turn.

Rnd 1: Ch 2, (sc in center of ring, ch 1) 9 times, sl st in first ch of beg ch-2.

Rnd 2: (Ch 3, work 1 mod 4 dc cl in next 2 sc st, ch 4, sl st in next ch) 5 times, end sl st in first ch of beg ch-3.

Rnd 3: [(Ch 3, sk next ch, hdc in next ch, ch 3, (dc, ch 2, dc, ch 2, dc) in the eye at top of cl, ch 3, sk next ch, hdc in next ch, ch 3, sl st in sl st bet petals], rep bet [ ] 4 times.

Rnd 4: Ch 4, (sk next st, sc in next st, ch 3) around entire flower, end sl st in first ch of beg ch-4 of this rnd. Fasten off.

Folded Flower Petal Motif B: Leave an 8" tail before beg for sewing. Ch 4, sl st in beg ch to form a ring, turn.

Rnd 1: Ch 2, (sc in center of ring, ch 1) 9 times, sl st in first ch of beg ch-2.

Rnd 2: (Ch 3, work 1 mod 4 dc cl in next 2 sc st, ch 4, sl st in next ch) 5 times, end sl st in first ch of beg ch-3.

gauge
finished Flower Motif A = 2½" in diameter

finished Folded Flower Petal motif B = 3" in diameter

special stitches
mod 4 dc cl

Rnd 3: [(Ch 3, sk next ch, hdc in next ch, ch 3, (dc, ch 2, dc, ch 2, dc) in the closing ch at top of cl, ch 3, sk next ch, hdc in next ch, ch 3, sl st in sl st bet petals], rep bet [ ] 4 times.

Rnd 4: Ch 4, (sk next st, sc in next st, ch 3) around 2 petals, ch 5, (sk next st, dc in next st, ch 3) around rem 3 petals, end ch 3, sl st in first ch of beg ch-4. Fasten off. Fold the 2 small petals in front of 3 large petals (RS tog) just below center of flower. Use the 8" tail to tack the folded petals thr the flower just above the center of flower.

Attach flowers to garment as desired.

nubby flowers

The contrasting group of flowers in this beautiful gold nubby yarn are a perfect accent to a simple brown poncho or sweater.

materials
- cotton/rayon yarn
- size F hook, or size required to obtain gauge

directions
Note: Model used 3 of 4-petal Motif A, and 3 of 5-petal Motif B.

4-petal Motif A: Ch 7, [(3 dtr, 2 tr, 1 dc) in beg ch of ch-7, ch 3, sl st in same st, ch 6], rep bet [ ] 3 times, work all 4 petals in same st as beg. Fasten off.

5-petal Motif B: Ch 7, [(3 dtr, 2 tr, 1 dc) in beg ch of ch-7, ch 3, sl st in same st, ch 6], rep bet [ ] 4 times, work all 5 petals in same st as beg. Fasten off.

gauge
finished motif = 3" in diameter

special stitches
dtr

84

peony flower

This soft flouncy flower is added to the wonderful ruffles of a pink sweater. The flower is fun to make and can be changed in so many ways to create new flowers for any use. Be certain to work loosely to ensure a ruffled, fluffy appearance.

materials

- silk/wool yarn
- size D hook, or size required to obtain gauge

gauge

finished motif = 4" in diameter

directions

Note: One flower motif takes a little more than 1 skein.

Ch 4, sl st in beg ch to form a ring.

Rnd 1: Ch 1, 12 sc in ring, sl st in first sc.

Rnd 2: (Ch 14, sl st in same st at base of ch, 2 sc in next st, ch 2, sc in same st, sl st in next st) 6 times.

Rnd 3: (Sk the ch-14 lp, sl st around post of the second sc in the next 2-sc group, ch 24, sl st in same st) 6 times.

Rnd 4: Sl st into ch-2 lp of Rnd 2, ch 1, 6 sc in same ch-2 lp, (6 sc in next ch-2 lp) 5 times, sl st in beg sc. Do not detach yarn. (1 flower center completed) Tie a knot in each of the ch-14 lps and ch-24 lps, keeping the knot at the top of the lp. *Note: Tying the knots now keeps the lps from getting in the way of the next rnds.*

Note: The next 2 rnds are foundation rnds to support the inner and outer petals.

Rnd 5: (Ch 4, sl st in same sl st at base of ch, ch 6, sl st in next sp bet 6-sc groups) 6 times.

Rnd 6: (Ch 6, sl st in same sl st at base of ch, ch 8, sl st in sl-st made in Rnd 5 bet next 6-sc groups) 6 times.

Rnd 7 (Inner Petals): Sl st to nearest ch-4 lp, ch 4, [(dc in same ch-4 lp, ch 1) 3 times, dc in first sc of 6-sc group made by Rnd 4, ch 1, dc in next st (second sc), ch 1, dc in same st, ch 1. Turn flower to WS. (Dc in ch-6 lp made by Rnd 5, ch 1) 3 times, turn flower to RS. (Dc in next (third) sc of 6-sc group made by Rnd 4, ch 1) 3 times. (Dc in same ch-6 lp made by Rnd 4, ch 1) 3 times. Turn flower to WS. Dc in fifth sc made by Rnd 5, ch 1, (dc in fourth sc made by Rnd 5, ch 1) 2 times. Turn flower to RS. Dc in sixth sc made by Rnd 5, ch 1,* dc in next ch-4 lp, ch 1], rep 5 times, end last rep at *. Sl st in third ch of beg ch-4, sl st in second ch of beg ch-4, sl st in first ch of beg ch-4, sl st in nearest ch-6 lp made by Rnd 6.

Rnd 8 (Outer Petals): Ch 5, [(tr in same ch-6 lp, ch 1) 5 times, (tr in ch-8 lp, ch 1) 2 times, turn flower to WS, (tr in same ch-8 lp left of previous tr, ch 1) 2 times, turn flower to RS, (tr in same ch-8 lp left of previous tr, ch 1) 6 times, rotate flower upside down, still on RS, tr in same ch-8 lp right of previous tr, ch 1, tr in same ch-8 lp left of previous tr, ch 1. Rotate flower right side up on RS, (tr in same ch-8 lp left of previous tr, ch 1) 2 times, tr in next ch-6 lp made from Rnd 6, ch 1] 6 times, ending with sl st in fourth ch of beg ch-5. Fasten off.

ribbon embellishments

round medallion

This simple little grey sweater has blossomed into a spring garden covered with pinks and greens. The individual flowers and leaves make up a colorful combination of silk ribbon, pearle cotton, and crochet thread. Have a wonderful time creating your own bouquet.

gauge
finished motif = 2½" in diameter

multitoned ribbon flower

materials

• #3 cotton crochet thread
• ¼"-wide silk ribbon
• size D hook, or size required to obtain gauge
• size G hook, or size required to obtain gauge

directions

Using size D hk and cotton thread, ch 3, sl st in beg ch to form a ring.

Rnd 1: Ch 2, (hdc in ring) 7 times, sl st in second ch of beg ch-2. Fasten off.

Rnd 2: Using size G hk and ribbon, join with sl st in any hdc, ch 1, sc in same st, ch 5, (sc in next st, ch 5) 7 times, sl st in beg sc. Fasten off.

materials

• ¼"-wide silk ribbon in color A
• ¼"-wide silk ribbon in color B
• ¼"-wide silk ribbon in color C
• size G hook, or size required to obtain gauge

directions

Using col A, ch 3, sl st in beg ch to form a ring.

Rnd 1: Ch 1, (sc in ring) 8 times, sl st in beg sc. Fasten off.

Rnd 2: Using col B, join with sl st in any sc, ch 1, (2 sc in next st) 8 times, sl st in beg sc. Fasten off.

Rnd 3: Using col C, join with sl st in any sc, ch 1, (2 sc in next st) 16 times, sl st in beg sc. Fasten off.

Rnd 4: Using col B, work in back lp only, join ribbon with sl st in any sc, ch 1, sc in ea st around, sl st in beg sc. Fasten off.

gauge
finished motif = 2" in diameter

streamers & loops

gauge
finished motif = 2½" in diameter

materials

- #3 cotton crochet thread in color A
- #3 cotton crochet thread in color B
- size G hook, or size required to obtain gauge

directions

Using col A, ch 3, sl st in beg ch to form a ring.

Rnd 1: *Note: Work in spiral, mark beg of rnd with safety pin and move it up after ea rnd is complete.* Ch 1, 4 sc in ring.

Rnd 2: (2 sc in next st) 4 times. Fasten off.

Rnd 3: Using col B, join with sl st in last sc worked, (2 sc in next st) 8 times.

Rnd 4: Work this rnd in back lp only, (sc in next st, 2 sc in next st) 8 times.

Rnd 5: Work thr both lps. Ch 1, sc in same st, ch 5, sc in same st, [(sc in next st) 2 times, (sc, ch 5, sc) in next st], rep bet [ ] 7 times, sl st in beg sc. Fasten off.

Streamers & Loops: Using col B, leave a 2" tail, make a slipknot to begin, ch 20, sl st in any st of Rnd 3, ch 12, leave a 2" tail, fasten off. Using col B, leave a 2" tail, make a slipknot to begin, ch 8, work 1 sl st in the st 2-sts to right of sl-st that attached last streamer, ch 20, sl st in same st, ch 14, sl st in next st of Rnd 4, ch 18, leave a 2" tail. Fasten off.

light & dark ribbon round

gauge
finished motif = 2" in diameter

materials

- ⅛"-wide silk ribbon in color A
- ⅛"-wide silk ribbon in color B
- size D hook, or size required to obtain gauge

directions

Using col A, ch 3, sl st in beg ch to form a ring.

Rnd 1: Ch 1, (sc in ring) 10 times, sl st in beg sc. Fasten off.

Rnd 2: Using col B, join with sl st in any sc, ch 1, sc in same st (sc in next st) 9 times, sl st in beg sc.

Rnd 3: Ch 3, dc in same st, (2 dc in next st) 9 times, sl st in third ch of beg ch-3. Fasten off.

gauge
finished motif =
1½" in diameter

ribbon & thread round

materials
- #3 cotton crochet thread
- ⅛"-wide silk ribbon in color A
- ⅛"-wide silk ribbon in color B
- size D hook, or size required to obtain gauge

directions
Using crochet thread, ch 4, sl st in beg ch to form a ring.

Rnd 1: Ch 2, (hdc in ring) 11 times, sl st in second ch of beg ch-2. Fasten off.

Rnd 2: Using col A, join ribbon with sl st in any hdc, ch 1, sc in same st, ch 1, (sc in next st, ch 1) 11 times, sl st in beg sc. Fasten off.

Rnd 3: Using col B, join with sl st in any sc, ch 1, sc in same st, ch 1, (sc in next st, ch 1) 11 times, sl st in beg sc. Fasten off.

textured ribbon flower

materials
- #3 cotton crochet thread
- ¼"-wide silk ribbon
- size D hook, or size required to obtain gauge

directions
Using crochet thread, ch 3, join with sl st to form a ring.

Rnd 1: Ch 3, (dc in ring) 11 times, sl st in third ch of beg ch-3.

Rnd 2: Work this rnd in back lp only. Ch 1, sc in same st, (ch 14,* sc in next st) 12 times, end last rep at *, sl st in beg sc. Fasten off.

Rnd 3: Work this rnd in front lp only of Rnd 1 in top of ea dc. Using ribbon, join with sl st in any dc, ch 1, sc in same st, (ch 5,* sc in next st) 12 times, end last rep at *, sl st in beg sc. Fasten off.

gauge
finished motif = 4" in diameter

ribbon streamers motif

materials

- ⅛"-wide silk ribbon in color A
- ⅛"-wide silk ribbon in color B
- size D hook, or size required to obtain gauge

directions

Using col A, ch 4, sl st in beg ch to form a ring.

Rnd 1: Ch 2, 11 hdc in ring, sl st in second ch of beg ch-2.

Rnd 2: Ch 3, dc in same st, (2 dc in next st) 11 times, sl st in third ch of beg ch-3. (24 sts) Fasten off.

Rnd 3: Using col B, join with sl st bet any 2 dc, ch 1, sc in same st, (ch 12, sk 6 sts,* sc bet next 2 sts) 4 times, end last rep at *, sl st in beg sc.

Rnd 4: Ch 1, sc in same st, (ch 14,* sc in next sc) 4 times, end last rep at *, sl st in beg sc. Fasten off.

Rnd 5: *Note: This rnd will look like a ch st covering sts already worked.* Using col B, work around the post of hdc in Rnd 1, join with sl st in any st, with RS facing sl st on top of work in ea st around, end sl st in beg sl st. Fasten off and pl long tail to WS of work.

gauge
finished motif = 2" x 2"

large ribbon round

materials
- ¼"-wide silk ribbon in color A
- ¼"-wide silk ribbon in color B
- size G hook, or size required to obtain gauge

gauge
finished motif = 3½" in diameter

directions
Using col A, ch 9, 12 sc to form a ring.

Rnd 1: Join with sl st, sl st in ea sc in ring.

Rnd 2: Join with a sl st, sc around post of ea sl st in Rnd 1. *Note: The post is the base of ea sl st, not using the upper part of the st shaped like a "V".*

Rnd 3: Join with a sl st, ch 1, sc in back lp of Rnd 2 st, ch 1, rep patt around.

Rnd 4: Join with a sl st, ch 4, dc, ch, dc, rep patt dc, ch to beg, sl st in top of ch-4. Fasten off, weave ribbon end in to back of motif.

Rnd 5: Using col B, ch 6, sc in ch st of Rnd 4, ch 6, rep around, fasten off at last sc.

small thread round

gauge
finished motif = 2" in diameter

materials
- #8 crochet thread in color A
- #8 crochet thread in color B
- size G hook, or size required to obtain gauge

directions

Using col A, ch 3, sl st in beg ch to form a ring.

Rnd 1: Sl st 18 times in a spiral, st 2 sc in ea sl st 10 times. Do not fasten off.

Rnd 2: Using col B, sc, 2 sc, sc rep patt to the beg of the col B addition. Do not fasten off.

Rnd 3: Pl col A to Rnd 2, rep the patt in Rnd 2 to the beg of col A.

Rep the Rnds 1–3 as many times as desired, pl the alternate col at the beg of ea col change. On the last rnd, pl the desired col and ch 4, sc in same st, sc, sc, ch 4, sc in same st. Rep patt until you reach the first ch 4, sl st in sc st and fasten off.

ribbon leaves

materials

- ⅜"-wide silk ribbon
- size G hook, or size required to obtain gauge

directions

Note: The leaves shown are all variations of this basic patt. The difference is made by the number of ch sts made at the beg, variation in the method of sc, hdc, and dc sts that fill out the leaf sides, and in the number of rnds completed.

Ch 13.

Rnd 1: Down one side of the ch, sc, sc, sc, hdc, hdc, dc, dc, hdc, hdc, sc, sc.

Rnd 2: Ch 1, cross over to the other side of the ch and rep the patt in Rnd 1.

Rnd 3: When you have reached the top of the leaf, you may sc around the leaf again and fasten off at the top, weaving the ribbon into the leaf back.

Variations:

Ch more than the indicated 13 ch to make a stem, then follow Rnds 1–3.

Add additional rnds of shaping using the sc, hdc, dc, and tr dc. Work the original shaping and rep as desired to enlarge the leaf. An alternative method is to rep Rnd 1 and sc up the other side and down around the shaped side.

gauge
finished motif = 1½" x 2"

gauge
finished motif = 1" x 3"

gauge
finished motif = 1½" x 2½"

linen corsage

This crazy flower is made up of two colors of linen thread, some metallic embroidery floss, and some white jersey ribbon. Lots of texture and lots of action. It is pinned on this jacket to give it a bit of pizzazz.

materials
- embroidery floss (6 strand)
- jersey tricot ribbon
- lightweight linen yarn in color A
- lightweight linen yarn in color B
- size F hook, or size required to obtain gauge
- tapestry needle

gauge
finished motif = 4½" in diameter

directions
Using col A, ch 4, sl st in beg ch to form a ring.

Rnd 1: Ch 1, 8 sc in center of ring, sl st in beg sc.

Rnd 2: Ch 3, dc in same st, (2 dc in next st) 7 times, sl st in third ch of beg ch-3. (16 sts)

Rnd 3 (Petals): Petal 1: Ch 20, dc in third st from hk, dc in ea of next 17 sts, sc in next dc of Rnd 2. Petal 2: Ch 13, dc in third st from hk, dc in ea of next 10 sts, sc in next dc of Rnd 2, continue around in same manner. Petal 3: Ch 17, work 14 dc along ch, sc in next dc of Rnd 2. Petal 4: Ch 19, work 16 dc along ch. Petal 5: Ch 11, work 8 dc along ch. Petal 6: Ch 16, work 13 dc along ch. Petal 7: Ch 14, work 11 dc along ch. Petal 8: Ch 17, work 14 dc along ch. Petal 9: Work 16 dc along ch. Rep from beg of Rnd 3. (18 petals) Fasten off.

Rnd 4: Using col B, join with sl st around post of any dc of Rnd 2, ch 1, 2 sc around post of same dc, (2 sc around post of next dc of Rnd 2) 15 times, sl st in beg sc. (32 sc)

Rnd 5: Work 32 petals as before in Rnd 3, vary petal length by ch from 10 to 20 sts for ea petal, as desired. Example: Petal 1: Ch 14, dc in third st from hk, dc in ea of next 11 sts, sc in next sc of Rnd 4. Work a petal and anchor in ea sc of Rnd 4. After completing 32 petals, sl st to first ch of beg ch-14. Fasten off.

Center of Flower: Thread tapestry needle with 6 strands of embroidery floss, leave a 2" tail on RS of work, take a small st in center of flower to anchor floss, make 1"–2" lp and anchor with small tight st, continue to make lps of various lengths until center is covered as you desire (approximately 18 lps), leave a 2" tail on RS and cut floss. Thread tapestry needle with jersey ribbon, make lps same as worked with floss (approximately 12 lps). Trim ribbon.

silk flower string scarf

A sheer top like this needs something light and airy as an accent. This string scarf is made from a wonderful hand-dyed silk ribbon. The ribbon is wound on a flat spool and comes in a variety of colors, with variations within the colors chosen. The ribbon is sewn together at places on the spool. You are invited to use the spliced areas as they appear or to cut the pieces apart, tie a knot with tails and use the ribbon in that way. You can also combine several spools of different ribbon colors, tying them together as you want to bring a lot of variety to the texture of the scarf. For this project, flowers were made and tied together at various lengths apart and extra ribbon was tied to the piece to give it even more action.

materials
- $7/16$"-wide silk ribbon in color A
- $7/16$"-wide silk ribbon in color B
- size K hook, or size required to obtain gauge

directions
Using col A, ch 6, sl st in beg ch to form a ring.

Rnd 1: Ch 1, 8 sc in ring, sl st in beg sc.

Rnd 2: Work this rnd in back lp only, ch 1, sc in same sc, (ch 8, sc in next sc) 4 times, leave a 5" tail for streamer. Fasten off. Continuing this rnd using col B, and leaving a 9" tail for streamer, join with sl st in same sc (where previously fastened off), ch 1, sc in same st, (ch 8, sc in next sc) 3 times, leave an 8" tail, fasten off.

Finishing: Cut a length of col B to 18". Using this piece, tie a knot in the sp bet first and last sts of Rnd 1, tie a bow and leave ends as streamers.

gauge
finished motif = 4" in diameter

half-circle motif

This project shows the possibilities of combining vintage crochet pieces with brand new pieces. The center half-circle on this charming sundress was made to mimic two larger halves of a salvaged vintage doily. The pattern was copied by sight and the piece was made with fine crochet thread in matching colors.

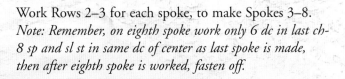

materials

• cotton crochet thread in color A

• cotton crochet thread in color B

• size 4 steel hook, or size required to obtain gauge

gauge

finished motif = 2½" x 4"

special stitches

mod puff st

directions

Using col A, ch 6, sl st in beg ch to form a ring.

Rnd 1 (Center): Ch 4, (dc in center of ring, ch 1) 15 times, sl st in third ch of beg ch-4.

Row 1 (First Spoke): Ch 13, dc in sixth ch from hk, ch 1, sk next st, dc in next st, (2 dc in next st) 5 times, sk next dc of Rnd 1, sl st in next dc, turn.

Row 2 (Second Spoke): Ch 8, sk 6 dc of first spoke, dc in next st, (ch 1, sk next st dc in next st) 2 times, leave rem sts unworked, turn.

Row 3 (Second Spoke cont.): Ch 4, dc in next dc, ch 1, dc in next dc, 10 dc in next ch-8 sp, sk next dc of center, sl st in next dc (spoke completed), turn, except on eighth spoke work only 6 dc in last ch-8 sp and sl st in same dc of center as last spoke made, then after eighth spoke is worked, fasten off.

Work Rows 2–3 for each spoke, to make Spokes 3–8. *Note: Remember, on eighth spoke work only 6 dc in last ch-8 sp and sl st in same dc of center as last spoke is made, then after eighth spoke is worked, fasten off.*

Edging: Using col B, join with sl st in seventeenth ch of first spoke, ch 1, [3 sc, ch 3, 2 sc in corner sp, (2 sc in next ch-1 sp) 2 times, 3 sc up side of next dc], rep bet [ ] 6 times, 3 sc, ch 3, 2 sc in corner sp, sl st in next dc. Fasten off.

Raised Center: Rnd 1: Using col B, join with sl st in center of beg ch-6 ring bet any 2 dc of Rnd 1, ch 1, work 2 sc bet ea dc around, sl st in beg sc. Fasten off.

Rnd 2: Work this row counterclockwise, work in sides around 2 posts of 2 dc held tog, in Rnd 1. Using col B, join with sl st, around any 2 dc, make a mod puff st as follows: [(yo, insert hk under 2 dc, pl up thread) 3 times, yo, pl thr 7 lps on hk, ch 1 to close], rep bet [ ] 7 times, moving around center. Fasten off.

bright balloons

A bright jumper is made even livelier with the addition of a bunch of balloons. Tails are added to these simple round motifs, turning them into fanciful flights of color.

materials

- #3 cotton crochet threads in a variety of colors
- size D hook, or size required to obtain gauge
- tapestry needle

gauge

finished motif = 1½" in diameter at widest point

directions

Motif: Ch 8, sl st in beg ch to form a ring.

Rnd 1: Ch 1, (14 sc, 4 hdc) in center of ring, sl st in beg sc, ch 5, leave a 2" tail, fasten off. If joining motifs tog, leave a 6" tail for sewing.

Joining: Thread tapestry needle with tail of thread and sew tog where desired.

ruffled flowers

This is a simple hand-knit sweater that has been embellished with some ruffled flowers. For your project, the yarn for the flowers needn't be the same yarn as the sweater—any yarn of coordinating colors and similar texture will work. The edges of the flowers will naturally curl up a bit, which adds to the charm.

small ruffled flower

materials

• dk weight tubular yarn with shiny thread
• size E hook, or size required to obtain gauge

directions

Ch 4, sl st in beg ch to form a ring.

Rnd 1: Ch 1, 7 sc in ring, sl st in beg sc.

Rnd 2: Ch 1, sc in same st, (ch 6,* sc in next sc) 7 times, end last rep at *, sl st in beg sc. Fasten off.

gauge
finished motif = 1¾" in diameter

large ruffled flower

materials

• dk weight tubular yarn with shiny thread
• size E hook, or size required to obtain gauge

gauge
finished motif = 2¼" in diameter

directions

Ch 4, sl st in beg ch to form a ring.

Rnd 1: Ch 1, 8 sc in ring, sl st in beg sc.

Rnd 2: Work this rnd in back lp only. Ch 1, sc in same st, ch 1, (sc in next sc, ch 1) 7 times, sl st in beg sc.

Rnd 3: Work this rnd in back lp only. Ch 1, sc in same st, (ch 6*, sc in next sc) 8 times, end last rep at *, sl st in beg sc. Fasten off.

apron blocks

This is an example of an heirloom piece accented with wonderful granny squares on point. Made with crochet thread and bright colors, these squares look as though they are part of the original apron.

materials

- cotton crochet thread in color A
- cotton crochet thread in color B
- cotton crochet thread in color C
- cotton crochet thread in color D
- size 8 steel hook, or size required to obtain gauge

directions

Note: Make 10 blocks for apron.

Using col A, ch 4, sl st in beg ch to form a ring.

Rnd 1: Ch 1, 8 sc in ring, sl st in beg sc. Fasten off.

Rnd 2: Using col B, join with sl st in any sc, ch 4, dc in same st, ch 1, [(dc, ch 1, dc) in next st, ch 1], rep bet [ ] 7 times, sl st in third ch of beg ch-4. Fasten off.

Rnd 3: *Note: Work this rnd in back lp only.* Using col C, join with sl st in ch-1 before the joining sl st of Rnd 2, ch 4, dc in same st, [ch 5, sk next 4 dc,* (dc, ch 1, dc, ch 3, dc, ch 1, dc) in next ch-1 sp], rep bet [ ] 2 times, end last rep at *, (dc, ch 1, dc) in same st as beg sl st, ch-3, sl st in third ch of beg ch-4. Fasten off.

Rnd 4: Using col D, join with sl st in any ch-3 corner sp, ch 1, 3 sc in same sp, [ch 1, sc bet next 2 dc in next ch-1 sp, ch 1, 6 sc in next ch-5 sp, ch 1, sc in next ch-1 sp bet next 2-dc, ch 1, (3 sc, ch 3,* 3 sc) in next corner ch-3 sp], rep bet [ ] 3 times, end last rep at *, sl st in beg sc. Fasten off.

gauge

finished block = 1¾" x 1¾"

cotton butterfly & trim

Here is an example of accenting a sweater. A simple border is crocheted around the edges of this sweater, using a variegated cotton yarn ranging in hue from green to tan and everything in between. A butterfly with beaded wings ties the colors together.

materials
- cotton yarn
- size E steel hook, or size required to obtain gauge

gauge
finished motif = 2" x 2¼"

finished sweater trim length = 64"

finished sleeve trim length = 9⅝"

special stitches
dtr

directions
Ch 6, sl st in beg ch to form a ring.

Rnd 1: (Ch 3, 3 dc in center of ring, ch 3, sc in ring) 2 times, (ch 3, dc, tr, dtr, tr, dc, ch 3, sc) in ring 2 times, sl st in first ch of beg ch-3.

Rnd 2: Ch 1, sc in center of ring, [(ch 3, sk next st, sc in back lp only of next st) 3 times, ch 3, sc in center of ring], rep bet [ ], (ch 3, sk next st, sc in back lp only of next st) 3 times, ch 3, sc in same st, (ch 3, sk next st, sc in next st) 2 times, ch 3, sc in center of ring, (ch 6, sl st in ea of fourth, fifth, and sixth ch from hk, sl st in the sc just made in center of ring) 2 times, (ch 3, sk next st, sc in back lp only of next st) 3 times, ch 3, sc in same st, (ch 3, sk next st, sc in back lp only) 2 times, ch 3, sc in center of ring. Fasten off.

Sweater Trim: Ch 290, turn.

Row 1: Sc in third ch from hk, [ch 3, sk next 2 ch, (sc, ch 3, sc) in next ch, ch 3, sk next 2 ch, sc in next 2 ch], rep bet [ ] across entire ch.

Sleeve Trim: Ch 30, sl st in beg ch to form a ring.

Border: Row 1: Work same as Row 1 of sweater trim across entire ch, join with sl st. Fasten off. Sew in place on garment.

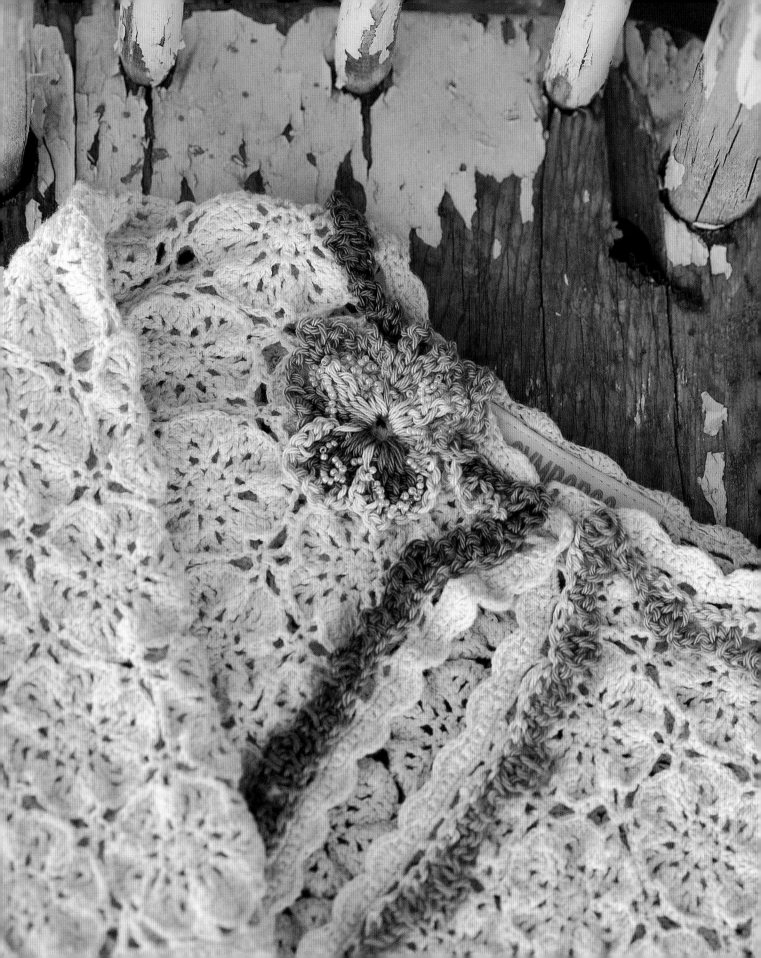

chapter 3:
granny square creations

The projects in this chapter are made entirely from granny squares. You'll be surprised at what cute, trendy projects they can make! From slippers to scarves to even T-shirts and skirts, granny squares can be combined to create just about anything.

cozy brown slippers

How luscious! These soft slippers are the perfect things to wear on a cool morning.

materials
- polyester "suede" yarn in color A (244 yds)
- polyester "suede" yarn in color B (122 yds)
- size K hook, or size required to obtain gauge

directions
Note: Use 2 strands of yarn throughout the patt. Make 2 oval blocks first, 1 for each slipper, as they are worked into the body of the slipper.

Oval Block: Using 2 strands of col B, ch 3, sl st in beg ch to form a ring.

Rnd 1: Ch 3, [hdc in ring, ch 1] 7 times, sl st in second ch of beg ch-3. Fasten off.

Rnd 2: Using 2 strands of col A, join with sl st in any ch-1 sp, ch 2, hdc in same sp, [2 sc in next ch-1 sp, 2 hdc in next ch-1 sp, (ch 1, dc) 3 times in next ch-1 sp, ch 1], 2 hdc in next ch-1 sp, rep bet [ ] once, sl st in second ch of beg ch-2. Fasten off.

Body of Slipper: Using 2 strands of col A, ch 18. (If smaller or larger size of slipper is desired, measure sole of foot from heel to toe in inches, multiply number of inches by 2 = number of ch.)

gauge
finished oval block = 3" x 4"

Note: Slipper fits ladies sizes 8–10. Pattern gives directions to change size of slipper body/sole for other sizes.

slipper body gauge: 2 sts = 1"

special stitches
2 dc cl

2-in-1 hdc (dec)

2-in-1 sc (dec)

3 dc cl

afghan st

Continued on page 112

Continued from page 110

Rows 1–6: Work afghan st. (If narrower or wider width of slipper sole is desired, work afghan st until the proper sole width is achieved.)

Row 7: Ch 1, work sl st in front bars of ea st to fill in the gaps of the afghan sts.

Note: Rows 8–12 are not worked around the slipper.
Row 8: Work 1 sc in corner st. At corner, rotate the block 90° clockwise, working along the width edge of the slipper, hdc along side of ea st until the next corner is reached, work sc in the corner st, rotate the block 90° clockwise, working along the length edge of the slipper, sc in ea st until the next corner is reached, rotate the block 90° clockwise, working along the width edge of the slipper, hdc along side of ea st until the next corner is reached, work sc in the corner st, rotate the block 90° clockwise, working along the length edge of the slipper, sc in ea st until the beg is reached, sl st in beg corner sc.

Row 9: Ch 1, on this rnd work sc all around, except when working along the width (heel and toe) edges of the slipper work sc in the first and last hdc of the heel and toe edges and hdc in the center hdc sts.

Row 10 (Toe and Heel Shaping): Ch 2, (work a 2 dc cl over next 2 hdc sts to make a dec) 2 times or until all hdc sts have been worked (heel is shaped), dc in ea of next sc sts, (work a 2 dc cl using next 2 hdc sts) 2 times or until all hdc sts have been worked (toe is shaped), dc in ea of next sc sts until beg, sl st in second ch of beg ch-2. Turn the shaped slipper to RS. *Note: From bird's eye view, you are working clockwise around slipper opening.*

Position the oval block so the center dc of the 3-dc group is at the center of the toe in the slipper body. Mark the center sts on both pieces with safety pins or yarn pieces. Locate the side points on the slipper body and the oval block where they will be attached tog and mark them with safety pin or yarn pieces.

Row 11 (Attaching the Oval Block): Ch 1, sc around heel until you get to the first attachment point (tenth st past the heel dec sts if patt size has not been changed), sc in the marked slipper body st, remove hk, pl up lp thr marked hdc oval block st, ch 1, [sc in next slipper st, remove hk, pl up lp thr next oval block st, ch 1] 3 times,

work a 2-in-1 sc using next 2 slipper body sts, remove hk, pl up lp thr next oval block (hdc) st, ch 1, work a 2-in-1 sc using next 2 slipper body sts, remove hk, pl lp up thr next oval block (ch) st, ch 1, work a 2-in-1 hdc using next 2 slipper body sts, remove hk, pl up lp thr next oval block (dc) st, ch 1, work 2 dc cl using next 2 slipper body sts, remove hk, pl up lp thr next oval block (ch) st, ch 1, work 3 dc cl using next center 3 (more or less depending on size of slipper) slipper body sts (center of toe), remove hk, pl up lp thr next oval block st (toe center dc), ch 1, work 2 dc cl using next 2 slipper body sts, remove hk, pl up lp thr next oval block (ch) st, ch 1, work a 2-in-1 hdc using next 2 slipper body sts, remove hk, pl up lp thr next oval block (dc) st, ch 1, work a 2-in-1 sc using next 2 slipper body sts, remove hk, pl up lp thr next oval block (ch) st, ch 1, work a 2-in-1 sc using next 2 slipper body sts, remove hk, pl up lp thr next oval block (hdc) st, ch 1, [sc in next slipper st, remove hk, pl up lp thr next oval block st, ch 1] 3 times, sc in the marked slipper body st (last attachment point—this is also the place that yarn will be joined to in the next rnd), remove hk, pl up lp thr the marked hdc oval block st, sc around to beg, sl st in beg sc. Fasten off.

Row 12: *Note: Work this rnd tightly.* Using 2 strands of col A, join with sl st in slipper body at last point that oval block was attached to slipper body in Rnd 4, pl up lp thr next unattached oval block hdc st, sc in ea of next slipper body sts to st before center point of heel, work a 2-in-1 sc using next 2 slipper body sts, sc in ea of next slipper body sts to next oval block attachment point, pl up lp thr last unattached oval block hdc st. If high ankle cuff is not desired, fasten off; otherwise turn.

Rows 13–18 (High Ankle Cuff): Sc in ea sc st of previous rnd, turn, except after Row 11 fasten off.

Tassels: Make 2 tassels for ea slipper. Cut 8 strands from yarn to 6" long. *Note: Model used 4 strands of ea col.* Cut 2 strands to 8" long. Tie each tassel in the middle with an 8" strand. Pl up the ends of the tassel ties thr the desired place in the oval square and anchor underneath.

denim-colored poncho

It is hard to imagine that the square shown turns into a fun cover-up! This blue poncho is so comfortable both in its look and its feel.

materials
- acrylic/rayon/polyamide medium weight yarn (600 yds)
- size H hook (for neck opening), or size required to obtain gauge
- size S hook (body of poncho), or size required to obtain gauge

directions
Note: Make 24 blocks.

Using size S hk, ch 4, sl st in beg ch to form a ring.

Rnd 1: Ch 3, 2 dc in ring, ch 3, (3 dc in ring, ch 3) 3 times, sl st in third ch of beg ch-3, turn, sl st in ea of the first 2 ch to position hk at middle of ch-3 lp, turn.

Rnd 2: Ch 3, 2 dc in ch-3 lp, [ch 1, sk 1 dc and work 3 dc in center dc, ch 1, 3 dc in ch-3 lp], ch 3, 3 dc in same ch-3 lp, rep bet [ ], ch 3, turn.

Rnd 3: Dc in ea of next 2 dc, dc in ch-1 sp, dc in ea of next 3 dc, [dc in ch-1 sp, dc in ea of next 3 dc], 3 dc in ch-3 lp, dc in ea of next 3 dc, rep bet [ ] 2 times. *Note: Last dc is actually in third chain of the ch-3.* Fasten off.

Continued on page 115

gauge
finished block = 7½" x 7½"

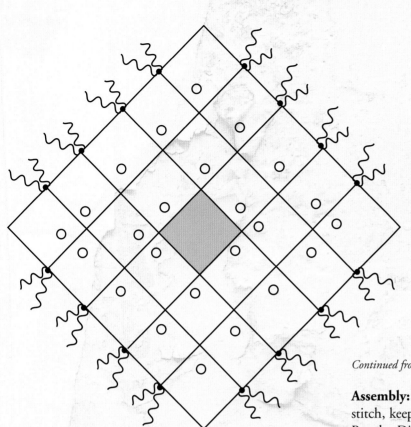

Poncho Diagram

Continued from page 113

Assembly: Arrange blocks tog and sew with the whip-stitch, keeping block "center rings" (shown as "o" in Poncho Diagram) toward the neck. *Note: The center "missing" square is the neck opening.* As you sew, knot the sewing yarn at each junction of blocks to stabilize the seams.

Fringe: If fringe is desired (shown in Poncho Diagram as wavy lines), leave a 6" length of yarn on the outer ends of the seams. Cut ea length of fringe to 12" and attach with larks-head knot at ea place fringe is desired. *Note: The model used 4 strands of yarn, ea 12" long, knotted at ea place that blocks met.* Trim fringe so it is uniform in length.

Finishing the Neck Opening: Using size H hk, join yarn at any corner of the neck opening with sl st. *Note: These rnds are worked to stabilize the size of the neck opening.*

Rnd 1: Work 15 sc along ea side of blocks at the neck opening as follows: 1 sc in ea dc top, 3 sc in ea ch lp, 3 sc in ea sideways dc, end with sl st in beg sc.

Rnd 2: Work 1 sc in ea sc st of Rnd 1, end with sl st in beg sc. Fasten off.

triangle shawl

This beautiful light floral shawl is the perfect weight for summer or an indoor winter setting. It is as cute as it is comfortable.

materials
- lightweight mohair blend yarn (396 yds)
- size F hook, or size required to obtain gauge

directions
Note: As motifs are made, they are joined to the shawl. Make 105 motifs.

First Motif: Ch 7, sl st in beg ch to form a ring.

Rnd 1: Ch 1, 12 sc in center of ring, sl st in beg sc.

Rnd 2: [Ch 10, sl st in next sc, (ch 8, sl st in next sc) 2 times], rep bet [ ] 3 times, sl st in first ch of beg ch-10. Fasten off.

Additional Motifs: Ch 7, sl st in beg ch to form a ring.

Rnd 1: Ch 1, 12 sc in center of ring, sl st in beg sc.

Rnd 2 (Joining Rnd): [Ch 5, sl st a ch-10 lp of First Motif, ch 5, sl st in next sc in Rnd 1 of second motif, (ch 8, sl st in next sc of Rnd 1 of second motif) 2 times], rep bet [ ] once in next ch-10 lp of First Motif, complete second motif as follows: [ch 10, sl st in next sc, (ch 8, sl st in next sc) 2 times], rep bet [ ] once, sl st in first ch of beg ch-10. Fasten off.

Finishing: Continue to add motifs in same manner, joining where necessary until there are 14 rows of motifs. Inc 1 motif ea row. There will be 14 motifs across last row worked.

gauge
finished motif = 3" x 3"

ribbon block skirt

You will find crocheted skirts in the fashion magazines, but not one like this. Lustrous silk is made up into individual rectangles and sewn together to make this lovely skirt.

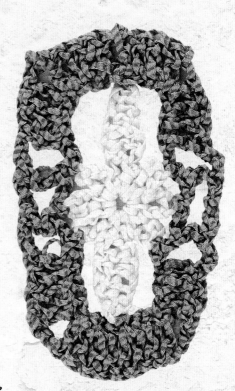

materials

- cotton/rayon ribbon in color A (103 yds)
- cotton/rayon ribbon in color B (206 yds)
- cotton/rayon ribbon in color C (103 yds)
- cotton/rayon ribbon in color D (103 yds)
- cotton/rayon ribbon in color E (103 yds)
- cotton/rayon ribbon in color F (103 yds)
- size H hook, or size required to obtain gauge

directions

Note: Make 48 blocks total; vary center and outside col as shown in Ribbon Block Diagram at right.

Using col A (center), ch 4, sl st in beg ch to form a ring.

Rnd 1: Ch 1, sc in center of ring, [(ch 5, sc in ring) 3 times, ch 8, sc in fourth ch from hk, hdc in next ch, dc in next 2 ch, hdc in next ch,* sc in ring (leaf made)] rep bet [ ], end last rep at *, sl st in beg sc. Fasten off.

Rnd 2: Working in back lp only, using col B (outside), join with sc in center ch of leaf point, [ch 8, (sc in center ch of next ch-5 lp, ch 3) 2 times, sc in center ch of next ch-5 lp, ch 8,* sc in center ch of leaf point], rep bet [ ], end last rep at *, sl st in beg sc.

gauge
finished block = 3" x 5"

Rnd 3: Ch 3, dc in next 3 ch, [ch 3 for corner, dc in next 4 ch, ch 2, sk next 3 sts, dc in next st, ch 3, sk next 3 sts, dc in next st, ch 2, sk next 3 sts, dc in next 4 ch, ch 3 for corner,* dc in next 8 ch], rep bet [ ] once, end last rep at *, sl st in third ch of beg ch-3.

Assembly: Referring to Ribbon Block Diagram below, whipstitch blocks tog thr back lp only. Leave bottom row of blocks free on three sides, joining them to skirt on top side only, like flaps.

C	E	D	D	D	A	B	E	A	F	E	B
F	D	A	C	E	C	A	F	D	C	A	C
E	A	C	D	F	B	A	F	C	B	C	F
B	E	B	F	B	D	C	D	B	F	B	B
E	D	A	F	D	C	C	E	C	E	A	D
A	B	C	E	A	F	F	B	A	C	F	E
C	F	B	F	B	B	E	D	F	B	A	B
E	D	F	B	E	E	D	B	E	C	B	D

Ribbon Block Diagram

118

light summer scarf

This light quick-to-make scarf is a perfect accent for spring or summer outfits.

materials

- cotton/polyester/viscose yarn (164 yds)
- size F hook, or size required to obtain gauge

directions

Note: Make 15 motifs, connecting them as they are made.

Ch 4, sl st in beg ch to form a ring.

Rnd 1: Ch 1, sc in center of ring, (ch 3, work 3 dc cl in ring, ch 4,* sc in ring) 4 times, end last rep at *, sl st in beg sc.

Rnd 2: Ch 8, [sc in top of 3 dc cl, ch 4,* tr in next sc, ch 4], rep bet [ ] 4 times, end last rep at *, sl st in fourth ch of beg ch-8.

Rnd 3: Ch 1, (5 sc in next sp, sc in next sc, 5 sc in next sp, sc in next tr (corner st)) 4 times, end sl st in beg sc. First motif only: Fasten off. Do not fasten off additional motifs—use Assembly instructions.

Assembly: Join as described in Joining Motifs on page 13.

gauge
finished block = 3" x 3"
finished scarf = approx. 52" long

special stitches
3 dc cl

ribbon block t-shirt

This T-shirt is so fun to wear over thinner T-shirt or a cami. The unique yarn feels so wonderful and soft and shows so much texture and color.

materials
• dk weight acrylic ribbon yarn (540 yds)
• size H hook, or size required to obtain gauge

directions
Note: Make 24 blocks.

Ch 4, sl st in beg ch to form a ring.

Rnd 1: Ch 1, (sc, 3 dc) 4 times in center of ring, sl st in beg sc.

Rnd 2: Ch 1, sc in same st, (ch 4, sk next dc, sc in next dc, ch 4, sk next dc, sc in next sc) 4 times, sl st in beg sc.

Rnd 3: Ch 4, [(dc, hdc, sc) in next lp, sl st in next sc, (sc, hdc, dc) in next lp),* tr in next sc], rep bet [ ] 3 times, end last rep at *, sl st in fourth ch of beg ch-4.

Rnd 4: Ch 1, sc in same st, ch 5, sc in same st (ch 5, sc in next sl st, ch 5, sc in same st, ch 5,* sc in next tr, ch 5, sc in same st) 4 times, end last rep at *, sl st in beg sc.

Rnd 5: [Sc in next sp (ch 3, sc in same lp) 2 times, (sc in next lp, ch 3, sc in same lp) 3 times], rep bet [ ] 3 times, sl st in beg sc. Fasten off.

gauge
finished block = 5" x 5"

uptown shrug

This elegant shrug is made of designer yarn with a wonderful texture and sheen for a chic "uptown" look.

materials
- lightweight cotton/polyamide/viscose yarn (4 skeins)
- size F hook, or size required to obtain gauge

gauge
finished block = 4 ¾" x 4 ¾"

Note: 1 skein of yarn makes 7 blocks.

directions
Note: Make 22 square blocks for wrap.

Ch 6, sl st in beg ch to form a ring.

Rnd 1: Ch 3, 5 dc in center of ring, (ch 5, 6 dc in ring) 3 times, end ch 5, sl st in third ch of beg ch-3.

Rnd 2: Ch 1, sc in same st, [ch 5, sk next 4 sts, sc in next st, ch 2, (3 dc, ch 3, 3 dc (corner)) in next lp, ch 2,* sc in next dc], rep bet [ ] 3 times, end last rep at *, sl st in beg ch-1.

Rnd 3: Ch 4, [6 tr in next ch-5 lp, tr in next sc, sk to corner sp, (5 tr, ch 3, 5 tr) in next ch-3 corner,* tr in next sc], rep bet [ ] 3 times, end last rep at *, sl st in fourth ch of beg ch-4.

Rnd 4: Ch 1, (sc in next 13 st to corner sp, 4 sc in next corner sp, sc in next 5 sts) 4 times, sl st in beg sc (18 sc bet corner sps).

Rnd 5: Ch 4, (sk next st, dc in next st, ch 1) 3 times, [sk next st, hdc in next st, (ch 1, sk next st, sc in next st) 2 times, ch 1, (sc, ch 3, sc) bet 2 corner sc, (ch 1, sk next st, sc in next st) 2 times, ch 1, sk next st, hdc in next st, (ch 1, sk next st,* dc in next st) 4 times, ch 1], rep bet [ ] 3 times, end last rep at *, sl st in third ch of beg ch-4. Fasten off.

Wrap Assembly: Arrange blocks as in Uptown Shrug Diagram at left. Whipstitch tog thr back lp only.

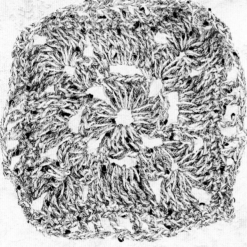

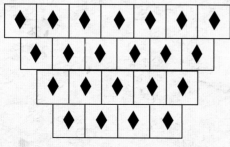

Uptown Shrug Diagram

seashells scarf

This scarf reminds me of shells on the beach and how the sea looks in a storm. I love the colors and textures. Imagine this also in a light multicolored yarn with long fringe.

materials
- acrylic/polyamide/wool yarn (213 yds)
- size K hook, or size required to obtain gauge

gauge
finished block = 7" x 7"
finished scarf = 7" x 52"

directions
Motif: Ch 17.

Row 1: Dc in fourth ch from hk and in ea rem ch across (15 dc), turn.

Rows 2–3: Ch 3, dc in ea st across, turn.

Row 4: Ch 4, (sk next dc, dc in next st, ch 1) 7 times (8 dc), turn.

Row 5: Ch 3, dc in next ch-1 sp, (ch 1, dc in next sp) 6 times, dc in third ch of tch (4 dc), turn.

Row 6: Ch 4, sk next dc, (dc in next sp,* ch 1) 6 times, sk next dc, dc in third ch of tch (8 dc), turn.

Row 7: Ch 3, (dc in next sp, dc in next dc) 7 times, turn.

Row 8: Ch 3, dc in ea dc across (15 dc), turn.

Row 9: Rep Row 4. *Note: If only making the motif, fasten off here. If continuing with the scarf, do not fasten off.*

To make the remainder of the scarf:
Rows 10–45: Alternate Rows 5 and 6 until 45 rows are completed from beg.

Rows 46–47: Rep Row 2.

Row 48: Rep Row 4.

Row 49: Rep Row 5.

Row 50: Rep Row 6.

Row 51: Rep Row 7.

Rows 52–53: Rep Row 8. Fasten off.

Fringe: Cut 32 strands at 16" long ea. Knotting 2 strands tog, make 8 fringes on ea end.

handbag

This is a classic purse that has been adapted and accented to show the variety that can be given to it with a little effort. A pocket has been added and a subtle trim added to the opening and strap. Imagine what a beautiful lining could do to further change the look.

materials

- crochet thread to match color A
- size H hook, or size required to obtain gauge
- tapestry needle
- worsted weight cotton yarn in color A (1 ball)
- worsted weight cotton yarn in color B (1 ball)

gauge

finished handbag = approx. 9" x 18" (shoulder strap not included)

directions

Note: Make 2, for one front and one back.

Using col A, ch 4, join with sl st in beg ch to form a ring.

Row 1: Ch 3, 7 dc in ring, turn.

Rows 2–3: Ch 3, dc in same st, 2 dc in ea rem st, turn.

Rows 4–5: Ch 3, dc in same st, dc in ea dc across to last st, 2 dc in last st, turn.

Row 6: Rep row 2.

Rows 7–10: Rep Row 4.

Row 11: Ch 3, dc in same st (dc in next st, 2 dc in next st) across, turn.

Rows 12–16: Rep Row 4, fasten off.

Shoulder Strap: Using col A, ch 220, turn.

Row 1: Dc in fourth ch from hk and in ea rem ch, turn.

Rows 2–5: Ch 3, dc in ea st across, turn, except after Row 5 leave a 10" tail, fasten off.

Thread tail into tapestry needle, whipstitch beg edge and ending edge tog to make a large ring.

Front Pocket: Using col B, repeat Rows 1–9. Leave a 36" tail for sewing pocket to front. Fasten off.

Assembly: Match beg center rings at top of bag opening and sew pocket to front of bag, matching centers of both pieces along bottom edge of pocket.

Place pocket-side of bag on top of back piece, matching edges. Pin shoulder strap with seam at bottom of bag to front piece of bag along one side of strap and back piece along other side of strap, making certain that both sides are aligned evenly across from ea other. Using col A, join with sl st thr both the front piece and the strap at one side of the bag at the top side edge. Work sc thr both the front and the strap pieces around the edges until you reach the opposite top edge of the front piece. Join other side of strap and back piece tog in same manner.

Trim: Using col B, join with sl st in first free st of bag, sc in ea st to joining of front and pocket, sc in ea st of front section to strap (work only thr the top edge of the bag, not including any of the pocket front at this time), sc in ea st along edge of strap to other side of front piece of bag, sc in ea st of front piece to pocket joining, work into top edge of pocket only, sc in ea st to end of pocket top, except work 5 hdc in ea beg ring of front, back, and pocket. Work along other side of strap and top edge of back piece, join with sl st in beg st of strap, sc in ea st along side of strap edge and ea st of top edge of back piece, join with sl st in beg st. Fasten off.

twine block & bag

Jute is the fiber of choice for this purse, which features squares around the bottom and a "netting" body. What a wonderful shopping bag this would make.

materials

• lightweight twine in color B (1 cone)
• medium to lightweight twine in color A (1 cone)
• size E hook, or size required to obtain gauge

directions

Note: Make 8 blocks for bottom of bag.

Using col A, ch 4, sl st in beg ch to form a ring.

Rnd 1: Ch 1, (sc in center of ring, ch 5) 4 times, sl st in beg sc.

Rnd 2: Ch 4, dc in same st, [ch 2, sc in next ch-5 lp, ch 2,* (dc, ch 1 dc) in next sc], rep bet [ ] 3 times, end last rep at *, sl st in third ch of beg ch-4.

Rnd 3: Ch 1, 2 sc in same st, [ch 2 (corner), 2 sc in next dc, 2 sc in next ch-2 sp, sc in next sc, 2 sc in next ch-2 sp,* 2 sc in next dc], rep bet [ ] 2 times, end last rep at *, sl st in beg sc. Fasten off.

Rnd 4: Using col B, join with sl st in corner ch-2 sp, ch 4, 2 dc in same sp, [(sk next st, dc in next st, dc in sk st) 4 times, sk next st,* (2 dc, ch 1, 2 dc) in next corner sp], rep bet [ ] 3 times, end last rep at *, dc in beg sp, sl st in third ch of beg ch-4.

Rnd 5: Sl st in corner sp, ch 4, 2 dc in same sp,* [dc in next 12 sts, (2 dc, ch 1, 2 dc) in next corner sp], rep bet [ ] 3 times, end last rep at *, dc in next 11 sts, dc in same corner sp as beg ch-4. Leave a tail for sewing. Fasten off.

Bag Assembly: With WS tog, join 8 blocks to form a ring with whipstitch thr back lps only. Fold in half. Whipstitch bottom of blocks tog.

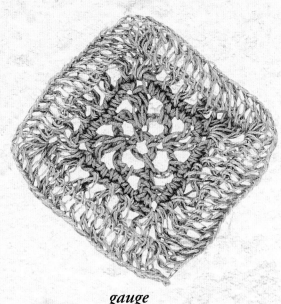

gauge

finished block = 3½" x 3½"

Top Edge Trim:

Rnd 1: Using col A, join thread to one side of top edge of bag with sl st, ch 1, sc in ea st around, end sl st in first sc.

Rnd 2: Ch 1, sc in same st [(ch 5, sk 3 sts, sc in next st) 3 times,* ch 5, sk 4 sts, sc in next st (have 4 ch-5 lps across ea block)], rep bet [ ] end last rep at *, ch 3, dc in beg sc.

Rnds 3–27: Ch 1 sc in same st, (ch 5, sc in next lp) around to last lp, ch 3, dc in beg sc.

Rnd 28: Work (2 sc, 3 hdc, 2 sc) in ea lp around, sl st in beg sc. Fasten off.

Bottom Edge Trim:

Row 1: Using col A, join thread in corner st with sc, [ch 5, sk next 3 sts, sc in next st, (ch 5, sk next 4 sts, sc in next st) 2 times, ch 5, sk next 3 sts, sc in joining st of blocks], rep bet [ ] across next 3 blocks, turn.

Row 2: Ch 1, work (2 sc, 3 hdc, 2 sc) in ea lp across, sl st in last sc. Fasten off.

Cords: Make 2 cords, each 16-ply twisted cord, 60" finished. Use 8 strands col A and 8 strands col B.

Finishing: With 1 cord beg at one side, weave cord over 2 mesh and under 2 mesh, around entire opening of bag. Weave rem cord beg at opposite side in same manner.

homespun classic

With openwork hexagon motifs, this throw is an example of how intricate and beautiful these granny squares can be.

materials

- sport weight cotton in color A (805 yds)
- sport weight cotton in color B (690 yds)
- sport weight cotton in color C (1,150 yds)
- size E crochet hook, or size required to obtain gauge

gauge

large motif = 9" in diameter

finished throw = approx. 44" x 44"

directions

Note: Since large motifs are joined while working Rnd 10, work motifs in rows according to Homespun Placement Diagram on page 135. Begin with First Motif in lower left-hand corner of diagram.

Large Motif:

First Motif (make 25):

Rnd 1: Using col A, ch 8, dc in first ch, (ch 4, dc in same st) 2 times, ch 4, sl st in fourth ch of beg ch-8 (4 sps around).

Rnd 2: Sl st into next sp, ch 3 for first dc, (2 dc, ch 2, 3 dc) in same sp, *ch 2, (3 dc, ch 2, 3 dc) next sp, rep from * 2 times more, ch 2, sl st in top of beg ch-3. Fasten off.

Rnd 3: Using col B, join with sl st in ch-2 sp after sl-st, working in back lps only, ch 1, sc in ea dc and ch around, sl st in first sc (40 sts). Fasten off.

Note: For Rnds 4 and 6, carry col not in use around by working over it with the next group of sts. To change col, bring up new col as last yo of st in previous col.

Rnd 4: Using col A, join with sl st in last rnd-3 sc, working in back lps only, ch 1, sc in next st, ch 2, sc in next st, *sc in next st, join col C and work (sc, 5 dc, sc) in next st (shell made). Using col A, sc in ea of next 2 sts, ch 2, sc in next st, rep from * around, sl st in first sc. Fasten off.

Rnd 5: Using col A, sl st into next ch-2 sp, ch 8 for first dc and ch 5, dc in same sp, *dc in next st, ch 1, sk across sc-shell-sc group, dc in next st, (dc, ch 5, dc) in next ch-2 sp, rep from * around, sl st in third ch of beg ch-8.

Rnd 6: Using col A, sl st into next ch-5 sp, ch 1 (2 sc, ch 3, 2 sc) in same sp, *join col C and work a shell in next dc, sk 1 st. Using col A, work 3 sc in next sp, sk 1 st. Using col C, work a shell in next dc. Using col A, work (2 sc, ch 3, 2 sc) in next ch-5 sp, rep from * around, sl st in first sc. Fasten off col C.

Rnd 7: Using col A, sl st into next ch-3 sp, ch 4 for first dc and ch 1, dc in same sp, *dc in ea of next 2 sts, ch 1, sk next shell and sc, dc in next sc, ch 1, sk next sc and shell, dc in ea of next 2 sc, (dc, ch 1, dc) in next ch-3 sp, rep from * around, sl st in third ch of beg ch-4.

Rnd 8: Sl st into next ch-1 sp, ch 5 for first tr and ch 1, 2 tr in same sp, *tr in next st, dc in ea of next 2 sts, dc in next sp, hdc in next st, dc in next sp, dc in ea of next 2

Continued on page 135

Continued from page 132

sts, tr in next st, (2 tr, ch 1, 2 tr) in next ch-1 sp, rep from * around, end with tr in same sp as beg, sl st in fourth ch of beg ch-5. Fasten off.

Rnd 9: Using col C, join with sl st in any ch-1 sp, ch 1, *sc in ea of next 13 sts, (sc, ch 1, sc) in next ch-1 sp, rep from * around, sl st in first sc. Fasten off.

Rnd 10: Using col B, join with sl st in any ch-1 sp, ch 6 for first dc and ch 3, dc in same sp, ch 1,* sk 1 st, dc in ea of next 13 sts, ch 1, sk 1 st, (dc, ch 3, dc) in next ch-1 sp, ch 1, rep from * around, end with sl st in third ch of beg ch-4. Fasten off.

Second Motif: Rep Rnds 1–9 as for First Motif, using col according to Homespun Placement Diagram and Homespun Table.

Rnd 10 (Joining Rnd): Join col for rnd 10 with sl st in any ch-1 sp, ch 6 for first dc and ch 3, dc in same sp, ch 1, *sk 1 st, dc in ea of next 13 sts, ch 1, sk 1 st (dc, ch 3, dc) in next ch-1 sp, ch 1, rep from * 4 times, ch 1, sk 1 st, dc in ea of next 13 sts, ch 1, sk 1 st, dc in next ch-1 sp, ch 1, sc in ch-3 sp on First Motif, [ch 1, dc in same sp on Second Motif, ch 1, sk 1 st, dc in ea of next 13 sts, ch 1, sk 1 st], dc in next ch-1 sp, ch 1 sc in next ch-3 sp on First Motif, rep bet [ ] once, sl st in third ch of beg ch- 6. Fasten off.

Rep Rnds 1–10 on page 132 and above, according to Homespun Placement Diagram and using col as shown on Homespun Table. *Note: Make the number of ea motif as shown in parentheses.*

Homespun Placement Diagram

	Homespun Table				
Motif	**Rnds 1–2**	**Rnd 3**	**Rnds 4–8**	**Rnd 9**	**Rnd 10**
I (5)	Col A	Col B	Col A/Col C shells	Col C	Col B
II (6)	Col A	Col C	Col B/Col C shells	Col C	Col A
III (6)	Col A	Col B	Col C/Col B shells	Col B	Col A
IV (4)	Col B	Col C	Col A/Col C shells	Col C	Col B
V (4)	Col B	Col A	Col C/Col A shells	Col A	Col B

Small Motif (make 16): *Note: Small Motifs are joined in the openings bet rows of Large Motifs.*

Rnds 1–3: Using col C, rep Rnds 1–3 of Large Motif on page 132.

Rnd 4 (Joining Rnd): (Sc, 5 dc, sc) in next st, sl st in next st,* ch 6, sc in joining sc of 2 Large Motifs, ch 6, sk 2 sts on Small Motif, sl st in next st, (sc, 5 dc, sc) in next st, sl st in next st, ch 6, sc in center st of 13-dc group on Large Motif, ch 6, sk 2 sts on Small Motif, sl st in next st, (sc, 5 dc, sc) in next st, sl st in next st, rep from * around, sl st in first sc. Fasten off.

Finishing: Continue to make and join small motifs as established.

woven rings

materials
- ½"-diameter cord (1¾ yds)
- worsted weight acrylic yarn in color A (2,200 yds)
- worsted weight acrylic yarn in color B (2,090 yds)
- worsted weight acrylic yarn in color C (1,650 yds)
- size F crochet hook, or size required to obtain gauge

gauge
block = 16"

finished afghan = approx. 48" x 80" (not including edging)

special stitches
pc

directions
Afghan square (make 15):
Ring 1: Using col A, ch 22, join with a sl st to form a ring. Ch 1, 40 sc in ring, sl st in beg ch-1. Fasten off.

Ring 2: Using col B, ch 22 st ch thr first ring (keep RS of rings up), join with a sl st to form a ring. Ch 1, 40 sc in ring, sl st in beg ch-1. Fasten off.

Rings 3–7: Make 5 more rings as established, alternating col A and col B and joining thr previous ring as established until there are 7 rings ending with a col A ring.

Ring 8: Using col B, make another ring as established, joining thr first and seventh rings.

Ring 9: Using col C, ch 20. Lay 8-ring square flat with RS up. Ring 9 is the center joining ring and is woven thr col A rings as follows: Sl col C ch under first and third rings, over third and fifth rings, under fifth and seventh rings, and over seventh and first rings. Join with sl st in first ch of ch-20 to form a ring. Ch 1, 40 sc in ring, sl st in beg ch-1. Fasten off. Work rem of square around woven rings.

Rnd 1: Beg with a col B ring in any corner, join col B with a sl st in any sc, ch 4 for first dc and ch 1, sk 1 st, dc in next st, (ch 1, sk 1 st, dc in next st) 2 times, ch 1, sk 1 st,* [(dc, ch 3, dc) in next st for corner, (ch 1, sk 1 st, dc in next st) 4 times (10 dc in col B corner ring). Ch 1, working in next col A ring, dc in any sc, (ch 1, sk 1 st, dc in next st) 4 times (5 dc in col A ring). Ch 1*, working in next corner ring, dc in any sc, ch 1, sk 1 st, (dc in next st, ch 1, sk 1 st) 3 times], rep bet [ ] 3 times, end last rep at *, sl st in third ch of beg ch-4.

Rnd 2: Ch 1, *sc in ea dc and ch to next corner, work 2 sc in first ch at corner, 3 sc in center ch, sc in third ch of corner sp, rep from * around (140 sc around), sl st in beg ch-1. Fasten off.

Rnd 3: Using col B, join with a sl st in any corner, ch 3 for first dc, (dc, ch 3, 2 dc) in same st for corner, *(ch 2, sk 2 sts, dc in ea of next 2 sts) 8 times, ch 2, sk 2 sts, (2 dc, ch 3, 2 dc) in next st for corner, rep from * around, sl st in top of beg ch-3.

Rnd 4: Ch 1, *sc in ea st to next corner, work 3 sc in center ch of corner, 2 sc in next ch of corner, rep from * around (176 sc around), sl st in beg ch-1. Fasten off.

Continued on page 138

Continued from page 136

rep from * around, sl st in top of beg ch-3. Fasten off.

Rnd 7: Using col B, join with a sl st in any corner, ch 3 for first dc, (dc, ch 3, 2 dc) in corner sp, *ch 1, sk 1 dc of corner, dc in next dc of corner, (ch 1, pc in next dc, ch 1, dc in pc) 11 times, ch 1, pc in next dc, ch 1, dc in first dc of corner, ch 1, (2 dc, ch 3, 2 dc) in corner sp, rep from * around, sl st in top of beg ch-3. Fasten off.

Rnd 8: Using col A, join with sc in center ch of any corner, ch 7, sl st in sixth ch from hk, (ch 5, sl st in same st) 2 times, sc in same st as first sc (corner clover made), *ch 4, sk 2 dc of corner, sc in next dc, [ch 3, sc in next dc bet pcs, ch 6, sl st in sixth ch from hk, (ch 5, sl st in same st 2 times, sc in same dc (clover made), ch 3, sc in next dc] 6 times, ch 4, work corner clover in center ch of corner, rep from * around, sl st in first sc. Fasten off.

Rnd 9: Using col C, join with a sl st in center lp of any corner clover, *ch 12, sc in center lp of next clover, (ch 8, sc in center lp of next clover) 5 times, ch 12, sc in center lp of next corner clove, rep from * around, sl st in base of beg ch-12.

Rnd 10: Ch 3 for first dc, 2 dc in same st, *dc in ea st to next corner, 3 dc in corner, rep from * around, sl st in top of beg ch-3. Fasten off.

Rnd 5: Using col A, join with a sl st in any corner, ch 3 for first dc, (dc, ch 3, 2 dc) in same st for corner, *(ch 1, sk 1 st, dc in next st, ch 1, sk 1 st, work 5 dc in next st drop last lp from hk, insert hk in first dc of group, pick up dropped lp and pl thr to close pc) 10 times, ch 1, sk 1 st, dc in next st, ch 1, sk 1 st, (2 dc, ch 3, 2 dc) in corner, rep from * around, sl st in top of beg ch-4. Fasten off.

Rnd 6: Using col C, join with a sl st in any corner, ch 3 for first dc, (dc, ch 3, 2 dc) in corner sp, *ch 1, sk 1 dc of corner, dc in next dc of corner, (ch 1, pc in next dc, ch 1, dc in pc) 10 times, ch 1, pc in next dc, ch 1, dc in first dc of corner, ch 1, (2 dc, ch 3, 2 dc (in corner sp)),

Rnd 11: Using col B, join with a sl st in any corner, ch 3 for first dc, (dc, ch 3, 2 dc) in same st for corner, *ch 1, sk 1 st of corner, dc in next dc, (ch 1, sk 1 st, pc in next st, ch 1, sk 1 st, dc in next st) 17 times, ch 1, sk 2 sts, (2 dc, ch 3, 2 dc) in corner, rep from * around, sl st in top of beg ch-3. Fasten off.

Rnd 12: Using col A, join with a sl st in any corner, ch 3 for first dc, (dc, ch 3, 2 dc) in same sp for corner, *dc in ea st to next corner, (2 dc, ch 3, 2 dc) in corner sp, rep from * around, sl st in top of beg ch-3. Fasten off.

Assembly: *Note: Afghan is 3 squares wide and 5 squares long. Be certain that all center col C rings slant in the same direction.* Holding 2 squares with WS facing and working thr both pieces, join col A with a sl st in corner, *ch 1, sk 1 st, sl st in back lp only of next st, rep from * to next corner, continue joining squares as established for a row of 5 squares. Make 2 more rows of 5 squares ea. Join rows as established.

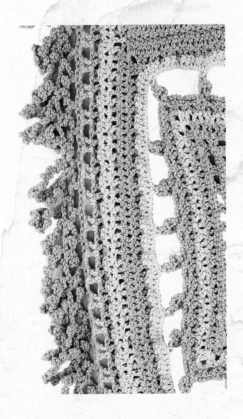

Edging:

Rnd 1: With RS facing and afghan turned to work across short edge, join col C with a sl st at corner, ch 3 for first dc, (dc, ch 3, 2 dc) in same corner, *(ch 1, sk 1 st, pc in next st, ch 1, sk 1 st, dc in next st) 15 times, ch 1, sk 1 st, pc in next st, ch 1, dc in joining, rep from * to next corner, omit last dc of last rep, (2 dc, ch 3, 2 dc) in corner sp, continue as established around afghan, sl st in top of beg ch-3.

Rnd 2: Sl st into ch-3 sp, ch 3 for first dc, (dc, ch 3, 2 dc) in same corner, *dc in ea st to next corner, (2 dc, ch 3, 2 dc) in corner sp, rep from * around, sl st in top of beg ch-3. Fasten off.

Rnd 3: Using col A, join with a sl st in any corner, ch 3 for first dc, (dc, ch 3, 2 dc) in same corner, ch 1, sk 1 st, dc in next st, *(ch 1, sk 1 st, pc in next st, ch 1, sk 1 st, dc in next st) to next corner, ch 1, sk 2 dc, (2 dc, ch 3, 2 dc) in corner sp, ch 1, sk 1 st, dc in next st, rep from * around, sl st in top of beg ch-3. Fasten off.

Rnd 4: Using col C, join with a sl st in any corner sp, ch 3 for first dc, (dc, ch 3, 2 dc) in same corner, *dc in ea of next 2 sts, (ch 2, sk across to next pc, 2 dc in pc) to 3 dc before next corner sp, ch 2, sk 1 dc, dc in ea of next 2 dc, (2 dc, ch 3, 2 dc) in corner sp, rep from * around, sl st in top of beg ch-3. Fasten off.

Rnd 5: Using col B, join with a sl st in any corner, work 5 sc in same corner, *sc bet next 2 dc, 2 sc bet next 2 dc, (sc bet next 2 dc, 3 sc in next sp) to 4 dc before next corner sp, sc bet next 2 dc, 2 sc bet next 2 dc, sc bet next 2 dc, work 5 sc in corner sp, rep from * around, sl st in first sc. Fasten off.

Rnd 6: Using col A, join with sc in center st of any corner, *(ch 6, sl st in fifth ch from hk to make a picot) 3 times, ch 1, sk 3 sts, sc in next st (3-picot lp made), ch 9, sl st in sixth ch from hk to make a picot, ch 3, sk 3 sts, sc in next st (single picot lp made), rep from * around working a 3-picot lp before and after ea corner, sl st in first sc. Fasten off.

Rnd 7: Using col A, join with sc in center picot of next 3-picot lp, (ch 6, sl st in fifth ch from hk to make a picot) 9 times, ch 1, sc in same picot as previous sc (9-picot lp made), *ch 3, sc in picot of next single picot lp, make a 9-picot lp, ch 3, sc in center picot of next lp, make a 9-picot lp, rep from * around, working a 9-picot lp in center picot of ea lp, end with ch 3, sl st in first sc. Fasten off.

about the author

Susan Cottrell graduated from Weber State University in Ogden, Utah, with a degree in drawing and painting. She has never been far from the creative aspects that life allows and has discovered that art can be expressed with paint and canvas, fiber and threads, colorful fabrics, beads and bangles, yarns and hooks, and no limits. Ever since her grandmother taught her to crochet, she has loved the convenience of it, the fun stitches, and the shapes that can be created by just playing around with hooks and yarns. To Susan, using unusual fibers, ribbons, and yarns is like painting three-dimensionally.

Susan has been blessed throughout her life with a wonderful group of nurturing people, learning and growing from each one. Her loving grandmothers, though very different, were both talented in the arts of drawing, painting, knitting, and crochet. Her mother taught her how to sew everything from doll clothes to children's clothes to quilts, while her father's artistic influence consisted of his hanging some really ugly paintings in his office! Susan's sisters were and are great examples of artistic gifts channeled into many different areas, and her brothers have always been supportive.

Susan's husband of 37 years and her four children have always been supportive of her artistic nature, even when all her paints, paper, threads, fabrics and whatever else were strewn across the kitchen or studio. Susan is delighted to pass on her talents. She keeps a small easel, table, and chairs, along with boxes of paints, crayons and paper, in her studio for her grandchildren.

acknowledgments

I am indebted to my grandmother, who taught me how to knit and crochet when I was very young. I had seen this wonderful woman knitting and crocheting ever since I could remember, and it was a secret wish to be just like her. It took me years to come close to matching her skills in crochet, but I finally learned how and I have really loved to crochet ever since.

I have been most fortunate to know some wonderful women who are very accomplished in the art of crochet: Marlene Lund, Connie Brand, Verna Facer, and Christina May. All have contributed greatly to this book, and I greatly appreciate their creations and kind help. Marlene and Connie worked with all of the patterns to allow us to enjoy using them.

I want to thank Lisa Anderson, who really worked wonders beyond what one might expect from an editor. She is a very fine woman with a great sense of humor tucked into her most gracious and kind personality. The good souls at Chapelle have been wonderful friends, great supporters, and most talented individuals. Thank-you to all.

contributing designers

Connie Brand learned to crochet, embroider, and knit at a very early age from her needlework-master mother, Marlene Lund. Her favorite projects involve creating original designs. Now retired from a career in computer programming and technical support management, she has more time to garden, research family history, do home schooling, and enjoy creative pursuits such as contributing designs for this publication.

Marlene Lund has been interested in needlework since she was eight years old, when her grandmother and mother taught her to embroider and crochet. Since then, she has become an expert in many kinds of needlework including knitting, counted cross-stitch, filet darning lace, needlepoint, candlewicking, crewel embroidery, ribbon embroidery, and Brazilian embroidery. She loves to create and share her talents, and has been teaching needlework classes for over 35 years at department stores, local yarn shops, and various continuing education programs. Marlene has previously designed patterns for Chapelle and the Vanessa Ann Collection, and has been published in *Better Homes and Gardens*. Marlene is also a professional dancer and enjoys golf and bowling.

Verna Facer was born and raised in the Ogden, Utah, area. She has belonged to a crochet/knitting group for more than 20 years. She also works and teaches at a knitting shop in Ogden. She has always enjoyed creating things in her own way and considers herself very lucky to be surrounded by so many talented people.

metric conversion chart

INCHES TO MILLIMETERS AND CENTIMETERS

inches	mm	cm	inches	cm	inches	cm
⅛	3	0.3	9	22.9	30	76.2
¼	6	0.6	10	25.4	31	78.7
⅜	10	1.0	11	27.9	32	81.3
½	13	1.3	12	30.5	33	83.8
⅝	16	1.6	13	33.0	34	86.4
¾	19	1.9	14	35.6	35	88.9
⅞	22	2.2	15	38.1	36	91.4
1	25	2.5	16	40.6	37	94.0
1¼	32	3.2	17	43.2	38	96.5
1½	38	3.8	18	45.7	39	99.1
1¾	44	4.4	19	48.3	40	101.6
2	51	5.1	20	50.8	41	104.1
2½	64	6.4	21	53.3	42	106.7
3	76	7.6	22	55.9	43	109.2
3½	89	8.9	23	58.4	44	111.8
4	102	10.2	24	61.0	45	114.3
4½	114	11.4	25	63.5	46	116.8
5	127	12.7	26	66.0	47	119.4
6	152	15.2	27	68.6	48	121.9
7	178	17.8	28	71.1	49	124.5
8	203	20.3	29	73.7	50	127.0

YARDS TO METERS

yards	meters	yards	meters	yards	meters	yards	meters	yards	meters
⅛	0.11	2⅛	1.94	4⅛	3.77	6⅛	5.60	8⅛	7.43
¼	0.23	2¼	2.06	4¼	3.89	6¼	5.72	8¼	7.54
⅜	0.34	2⅜	2.17	4⅜	4.00	6⅜	5.83	8⅜	7.66
½	0.46	2½	2.29	4½	4.11	6½	5.94	8½	7.77
⅝	0.57	2⅝	2.40	4⅝	4.23	6⅝	6.06	8⅝	7.89
¾	0.69	2¾	2.51	4¾	4.34	6¾	6.17	8¾	8.00
⅞	0.80	2⅞	2.63	4⅞	4.46	6⅞	6.29	8⅞	8.12
1	0.91	3	2.74	5	4.57	7	6.40	9	8.23
1⅛	1.03	3⅛	2.86	5⅛	4.69	7⅛	6.52	9⅛	8.34
1¼	1.14	3¼	2.97	5¼	4.80	7¼	6.63	9¼	8.46
1⅜	1.26	3⅜	3.09	5⅜	4.91	7⅜	6.74	9⅜	8.57
1½	1.37	3½	3.20	5½	5.03	7½	6.86	9½	8.69
1⅝	1.49	3⅝	3.31	5⅝	5.14	7⅝	6.97	9⅝	8.80
1¾	1.60	3¾	3.43	5¾	5.26	7¾	7.09	9¾	8.92
1⅞	1.71	3⅞	3.54	5⅞	5.37	7⅞	7.20	9⅞	9.03

index